HEROES *of* AMERICA™

Jackie Robinson

by Joshua E. Hanft

illustrations by Pablo Marcos

ABDO
Publishing Company

HEROES OF AMERICA™

Edited by
Joshua E. Hanft and Rochelle Larkin

visit us at
www.abdopub.com

Library edition published in 2005 by ABDO Publishing Company, 4940 Viking Drive, Suite 622, Edina, Minnesota 55435. Published by agreement with Playmore Incorporated Publishers and Waldman Publishing Corporation.

Printed in the United States.

Library of Congress Cataloging-in-Publication Data

Hanft, Joshua E.
  Jackie Robinson / by Joshua E. Hanft ; illustrations by Pablo Marcos.
    p. cm. -- (Heroes of America)
  Originally published: New York : Baronet Books, c1996.
  ISBN 1-59679-259-0
  1. Robinson, Jackie, 1919-1972--Juvenile literature. 2. Baseball players--United States--Biography--Juvenile literature. 3. African American baseball players--Biography--Juvenile literature. I. Marcos, Pablo, ill. II. Title. III. Series.

GV865.R6H36 2005
796.357'092--dc22

[B]

2004062654

Table of Contents

Important Dates

1919 Jackie Robinson born in Georgia

1920 Mallie Robinson and her children move to Pasadena, California

1936 Mack Robinson performs in Olympics in Berlin

1937 Jackie Robinson enters Pasadena Junior College

1939 Jackie Robinson enrolls in UCLA, excells in four sports

1942 Jackie Robinson enters the Army during World War II

1944 Jackie Robinson acquitted during court-martial trial

1945 Jackie Robinson plays for Kansas City Monarchs in the Negro Leagues

1946 Jackie Robinson breaks color line by playing for the Montreal Royals in the minor leagues; marries Rachel Isum

1947 Jackie Robinson's first year with the Brooklyn Dodgers, named Rookie of the Year

1955 Dodgers defeat Yankees to win World Series

1956 Jackie Robinson retires

1962 Jackie Robinson elected to Hall of Fame

1972 Jackie Robinson dies after long battle with diabetes

Chapter 1

The House on Pepper Street

"Take some of that energy of yours outside and do some chores," Mallie Robinson gently scolded her eight-year-old son. Jack Roosevelt Robinson was the youngest of her five children. Jackie, as his family called him, was always moving, running, jumping, playing ball; he had boundless energy.

Jackie picked up a broom and began to sweep the outside steps. The Robinsons lived in a house on Pepper Street, in Pasadena, California. It was a modest house in a neighborhood of working people,

The Only African Americans on the Block

but it was better than the crowded one the Robinsons had recently shared with Jackie's Uncle Burton.

There were problems, however, in their new neighborhood. The Robinsons were the only African Americans on the block, and Mallie and the children often encountered hate and prejudice.

In America in the 1920s, African Americans faced barriers and limitations to where they could live, where they could eat and where they could socialize. In the South, these limitations were known as Jim Crow laws. In the North, oftentimes, there were no laws that segregated white people from African Americans, but the silent barriers and limitations were there anyway.

For the Robinsons, living on Pepper Street brought them face-to-face on a daily basis with this unfortunate side of American life.

While Jackie was sweeping, a voice called out

suddenly, "Get out of our neighborhood. We don't want to see your black faces any more!"

Jackie felt anger boil inside him. No one worked harder than his mother, caring for five children and holding down a full-time job as a maid in order to have their house. No one should have the right to tell his family where they should live.

He saw a little girl, taunting and teasing, and found himself picking up a rock. He threw it at her. Before they knew it, the two children were in a rock-throwing fight.

Hearing the shouts, the little girl's father came out. He joined in—a grown man throwing stones at an eight-year old boy because of the color of his skin. Finally the little girl's mother came out to call her family back inside. Jackie, flushed, his chest heaving, rushed inside to his own mother.

"Child, what in the world was going on out there?" Mallie asked as she toweled off her

He Threw It at Her.

youngest.

"That little girl down the block was saying bad things about us again. So I chased her home with one of these." Jackie held up the rock in his hand. "If anyone says or does bad things about us because of our color, I'm gonna fight back."

Mallie smiled at her son. She had taught all her children to be proud that they were black, never to be ashamed of who they were or where they had come from.

"There's lots of ways of fighting back, Jackie," Mallie said softly. "Sometimes we have to defend ourselves with words and even our fists, but sometimes you can fight back just by ignoring that kind of ignorance and hate and showing people that you're proud to be, well, just *better* than they are."

"Not me, Mama, " Jackie answered. "I'll always fight back as hard as I can."

Jackie Robinson would think of this conversation twenty years later when he became the first African American to play baseball in the major leagues. For two years Jackie would hold his tongue and his fists, though he encountered unimaginable hatred and bigotry.

The courage that took was enormous, as Jackie became not just a professional athlete, but a symbol of his people. The pride and dignity he constantly showed made him one of the most admired athletes and all-around admired Americans in the twentieth century.

The eight-year-old boy filled with pride and anger on that sunny California day had no way of knowing what history had in store for him. In those early days, Jackie was just interested in playing sports and having fun.

From his earliest days Jackie Robinson showed great athletic talent. When sides were chosen, everyone wanted Jackie on his team. He excelled in

Jackie Had Learned to Compete.

whatever sport he picked up, from soccer, to handball, to foot races. As the youngest, Jackie had learned to compete from the time he was a child. And no one was more competitive than Jackie Robinson.

Jackie's family didn't come from California originally. The Robinsons had moved to California from Georgia. Jackie was born in Albany, Georgia, in a little log cabin on a plantation. Jackie's father, Jerry Robinson, was a sharecropper. After slavery was abolished in this country, a system of farming for black people in the South, called sharecropping, had developed.

A sharecropper would work the land for the owner of a plantation. In exchange for his work he would be given a cabin and some provisions. For all his labor, Jerry Robinson received the equivalent of three dollars' worth of food a week. The sharecropping system was only a small step beyond slavery. The owner of the plantation Jerry worked on, Jim

Sasser, was known for his great wealth, while the black sharecroppers barely had enough food for their families.

Mallie married Jerry Robinson in 1909. She immediately convinced him to ask Sasser to change Jerry's status from a sharecropper to a half-cropper. A half-cropper would give half the yield of his land to the plantation owner, and keep half for himself. Because Jerry was a good worker, Sasser agreed. Due to Mallie's efforts to have Jerry improve himself, the family income rose in one year from $134 to over $350.

Life, however, was difficult for the young couple. Jerry worked long, tiring days on the plantation while Mallie raised their five young children. The oldest, Edgar, was born in 1910, then came Frank in 1912, Mack in 1914, and a girl, Willa Mae, in 1916. Jackie, the youngest, was born in 1919.

Jerry Robinson had trouble handling his

Mallie Raised Their Five Children.

increased prosperity. He began spending more time in the town of Cairo and less at work on his farm. Suddenly he left, abandoning his wife and five children. Jackie was only sixteen months old at the time. He never knew his father.

Mallie Robinson was a deeply religious woman who wanted above all else to keep the rest of the family together. The South held little hope for her. The Ku Klux Klan was gaining in popularity in Georgia during the 1920s. The sharecropping system held no promise for a good future.

Her brother Burton had already moved to Pasadena, California and spoke of the greater opportunities there. Mallie made the brave decision to take her five young children and relocate to California.

It was a hard move to make, leaving behind family and friends, loading up all her belongings and five young children for the long and difficult train ride across the country. African Americans couldn't ride in the same compartments as whites; the segregated train was crowded and uncomfortable.

When they finally arrived, there were few job opportunities for Mallie. She became a maid, working long hours for little money. Often the children had only two meals a day, and one of the meals would be bread dipped in sugar water.

But the family was a close one. Each child had responsibility for taking care of the next younger one. Willa Mae, Jackie's older sister, would take baby Jackie to school with her, asking the teacher to let him play outside in the sandbox while she was at her lessons. If it rained, she would take him inside.

His oldest brother, Edgar, was in charge while Mallie was at work. Edgar was big for his age, and zipped around the neighborhood on roller skates, amusing his brothers. Like his mother, Edgar was deeply religious. Frank was serious and kindly.

A Cross Was Burned on Their Lawn.

Mack was strong and athletic. Young Jackie looked up to all his older siblings and admired them in different ways.

It was a close-knit family, held together by the religious training given to them by Mallie, brought even closer by the prejudice and hatred they encountered on a daily basis.

When the Robinsons first moved in, their neighbors tried to organize a petition to drive them out. Stones were thrown at them, their property was vandalized, and once a cross was burned on their front lawn. Edgar rushed to put out the fire.

Through all this, Mallie taught her children not to look for trouble, but not to be scared, either. The Robinson family stayed together. Looking back on his childhood, Jackie Robinson always remembered and appreciated the bravery and determination of his mother, and the warmth and support he got from his brothers and sister.

Chapter 2

The Pepper Street Gang

"Jackie, what are you doing? You know we're not supposed to sit here," whispered Jack Gordon to his friend.

The lights in the movie theatre had just gone down. Quick as a cat, Jackie Robinson had scrambled from his seat into the whites-only section.

"They won't pay any attention, now it's dark," Jackie whispered back. "Besides, we paid the same money, we should sit where we want."

"You're gonna get us thrown out again," Jack

"We Should Sit Where We Want."

cautioned his friend. "You know what happened last time."

Then the newsreel came on. News from all over the world, in 1934, was of little interest to poor fifteen-year-old black boys. But suddenly Jackie's eyes widened, as a film came on showing the professional debut of a black boxer named Joe Louis. Jackie couldn't stop himself from providing sound effects to go along with the exciting film.

With each punch landing, Jackie found himself shouting out, "Wham! Bam! Pow!" Here was a black man competing as an equal against whites and winning—a man of strength and power.

"What are you boys doin' here?" the usher whispered angrily, shining his flashlight on Jackie and his friend. "Get out and stay out!"

The two boys, laughing and joking, ran out of the theater, the usher chasing them.

"You'll never catch us," Jackie taunted as he

raced into the street. And no one could catch Jackie. He was the fastest kid in the neighborhood, except for his brother Mack, who was already a high-school track star.

Two blocks from the theater, Jackie and Jack stopped running and slapped each other on the back. They were both members-in-good-standing of the Pepper Street Gang, and liked to act up.

Despite Mallie's teachings, young Jackie Robinson had joined a street gang. Though their behavior was not very violent by today's standards, the gang did cause trouble. They would throw stones at passing cars, smash windows and raid local orchards. For tonight, they had even bigger plans.

"You know old man Carruthers, who's always calling us names? Let's pay him back," a gang member suggested.

"Why don't we put tar on his lawn!" said another.

That night, the boys of the Pepper Street Gang

His Destroyed Lawn

carried out their revenge. The next morning the boys laughed and whooped it up when from afar they saw old man Carruthers looking at his destroyed lawn.

They weren't whooping it up, however, when Mallie Robinson found out about it.

"What has gotten into your brain, child?" Mallie angrily confronted her son. "The Robinsons are not about spoiling other people's property, no matter what they say to us or about us. You get your friends and you clean up that mess."

Jackie felt torn inside. Part of him wanted to be a member of the gang, to belong to something bigger than just himself. He was also angry, like all the other members of the gang—angry that the black kids, the Mexican kids, and the Japanese kids were treated unfairly, often cruelly.

He was angry about having to shop out of special trucks, because he was not allowed into stores;

angry about being picked on by the teachers in school and accused of being the culprit any time there was a disturbance. He and his friends were tired of only being allowed to swim on Tuesdays in the public swimming pool, and that all the other days were reserved for whites only.

But another part of Jackie knew that his mother was right. Jackie spent hours and hours cleaning up old man Carruthers's lawn. Mallie insisted that all the sticky tar be cleaned up, one blade of grass at a time.

Still Jackie ran with the gang. One hot summer day, he and his friends scoped out a fruit store. When the owner's back was turned, Jackie grabbed some fruit and ran. As he rounded the corner in full flight, he felt a strong arm grab him around the waist.

The arm belonged to Carl Anderson, an automobile mechanic who was a friend of the family.

He Felt a Strong Arm Grab Him.

JACKIE ROBINSON

"What do you think you're doin', young man?" Carl shouted at the frightened boy. "Does your mama work all those hours, slavin' to the bone, washin' other people's clothes and houses, putting a roof over your head and food on your plate, for you to be stealin' and actin' up?" Anderson shook his head sadly.

"Jackie, you got a lot of good in you!" Anderson said seriously. "But you don't belong in a gang. You're followin' the crowd because you don't want to be thought of as different, of bein' chicken. But it takes real guts to do what's right, even when it's not easy. Boy, don't break your mama's heart."

Jackie felt ashamed to tell Carl Anderson that he knew he was right. From that moment on, Jackie knew his future was not with the Pepper Street Gang. But he still felt like he had no other place to be.

JACKIE ROBINSON

"Willa Mae, Edgar, Frank, Mack, Jackie...where is that boy?" Mallie sang out one bright Sunday morning. Sunday was the family's day to be together. The Robinsons always spent Sunday morning in church. Today was to be a special day. A new pastor, the Reverend Karl Downs, had come to the church.

Religion had always been a duty for Jackie. Unlike Edgar and Frank who were church-minded from the time they were young, Mack and Jackie had trouble keeping still in church. They would rather have been outside, running and playing ball. But today was different. They had never heard a preacher like Karl Downs.

Downs was a tall, red-haired African American, athletically built, in his early twenties. When he spoke he immediately had Jackie's attention. Downs was a young man, like Jackie, who knew what it was like to grow up black in a white man's world.

He Paid Special Attention to Jackie.

JACKIE ROBINSON

He preached with conviction and power. Pastor Downs had found his own peace in the church, and he wanted to help troubled teenagers by developing church youth programs and organizing team sports.

Downs sought out the kids of the Pepper Street Gang and talked to them individually and in groups. He paid special attention to Jackie. He sensed that Jackie had leadership qualities and saw his tremendous athletic potential. Pastor Downs knew if he could "recruit" Jackie Robinson, other kids would follow.

Eventually Jackie decided to be a volunteer Sunday-school teacher in Downs's church. The preacher counseled Jackie to leave the Pepper Street Gang and put his attention into team sports.

Jackie had always known he could jump higher and run faster than other kids, but when Pastor Downs showed him that he could concentrate his athletic skills into team and individual sports, his days as a member of the Pepper Street Gang were over.

Now his spare time was spent at practice and Jackie was learning one of the most important lessons of his life: he was finding out that discipline and hard work were as essential to winning as were the natural athletic skills he already knew he had.

His Days as a Gang Member Were Over.

Chapter 3

Athletic Success

"Go, Jackie, go!" Frank Robinson yelled out, urging his younger brother on. They were at the Muir Technical High School training track. Sports had become Jackie's passion and Frank was his biggest fan. Over the years Jackie and Frank had become extremely close.

Frank encouraged his younger brother and admired his athletic talent. Jackie looked up to Frank for his gentle nature and the kindness he showed to his brothers and sister.

JACKIE ROBINSON

As he grew and got stronger and faster, Jackie felt he was just beginning to tap his athletic potential. He always knew he was better at games than other kids. Even in grade school, kids would share their lunch with him just to get him on their team. But through the influence of Karl Downs, Jackie turned to competitive sports in junior high and high school, determined to win.

Jackie turned the anger and resentment he felt toward a prejudiced world into competitive fire. His driving nature was also fueled by someone closer to home—his brother Mack.

While Jackie was emotionally close to his brother Frank, he admired Mack's athletic ability. Mack was a junior-high, high-school, and junior-college legend. He was a gifted runner, basketball and baseball player. But in junior high he was found to have a heart murmur and was no longer permitted to play. Mack had Mallie go to the school to see if there was

Mack Set a High-Hurdle Record.

any way to allow Mack to compete. Finally an agreement was reached. Mack could compete in non-contact sports only, so he became a track-and-field star.

Mack Robinson set a statewide junior-high school high-hurdle record that lasted for many years. At Muir Technical High School, he was undefeated state champion in the 100-yard dash. At Pasadena Junior College, Mack continued his dramatic success, winning meet after meet at various events such as the 220, 440 and broad jump. More excitement was to follow.

"Wake up, sleepy head, it's gonna be time soon," Willa Mae whispered to Jackie early one morning in the summer of 1936. Jackie glanced at the clock. It was 2:30 A.M., and he hadn't missed it.

"Thanks for waking me." He smiled, kissing his sister on the cheek. "Is everyone up already?"

"They're all in the kitchen. It's so exciting!"

Jackie joined his family, huddled around the

kitchen table in front of the radio. Mack was in Berlin, competing in the 1936 Olympics. He was in the finals of the 200-meter dash. The Robinsons held hands as the announcer called the race:

"First out of the blocks is Mack Robinson; he is just flying. But here comes Jesse Owens. It's Robinson and Owens down to the wire. And it's Jesse Owens crossing the finish line."

A hush fell over the Robinson house.

"I'm proud of my boy!" Mallie Robinson finally said quietly.

"I'll never be proud to finish second," Jackie said aloud.

His brothers and sister looked at him, a little upset. But Mack would have understood. The fire of competition burned deeply within these two young men. Mack always felt he should have beaten Jesse Owens, but he made the mistake of looking back during the race. But while Mack was proud of his

"I'm Proud of My Boy."

silver medal, his Olympic experience was not a completely positive one.

Mack felt he should have been allowed to compete for a second medal in the 400-meter relay. But at the last minute, he and two other runners were replaced. The two other runners were Jewish and the United States Olympic Committee feared that the appearance of too many black and Jewish athletes could cause unrest in the host country, Nazi Germany. Mack was replaced by Frank Wyckoff, a slower white runner, who anchored the relay team so that a white man would appear at the finish line.

When Mack came home from the Olympics there were no ticker-tape parades, no trophies waiting for him. On his first night back, Mack had to stay in a different hotel than his white teammates because of the color of his skin.

The country he proudly represented didn't seem to take any pride in him. When he returned to

JACKIE ROBINSON

Pasadena, the only job he could find was as a street sweeper, working the midnight shift.

But Jackie's athletic career was just taking off. Following in Mack's footsteps, Jackie lettered in track at Muir Technical High. He also joined the school's football, baseball and basketball teams, becoming a four-letter man.

In basketball he led the team in assists, rebounding and scoring. His broken-field running on the football field was amazing to watch. He could play running back and quarterback. On the baseball field he could hit for power and run the base paths like no one else. On the track, he competed more against his brother's records than current opponents. Soon, it was on to greater challenges at Mack's old school—Pasadena Junior College.

"I can't believe it," Jackie Robinson groaned as the car rolled to a stop. His friend, Johnny Burke,

A Junior College National Record.

was driving. "A flat tire, man, we're never gonna make the meet."

Jackie and his friends hopped out of the car. The track meet was only about a half hour away, and if you were late you weren't allowed to compete.

Suddenly a car pulled up next to them. "What's wrong, boys?" a cheerful voice called out. It was John O'Mara, Dean of Students at Pasadena Junior College. Jackie and his friends explained. O'Mara offered his spare tire, which luckily fit. Happily, the boys jumped in and sped to the meet.

When they got there, Jackie did not even have time to take off his warm-up clothes, let alone loosen up. He was competing in the broad jump. Not having time to warm up would be devastating for most young athletes. But not for Jackie Robinson. On his fourth and final attempt, he jumped 25 feet, 6½ inches long. His jump not only broke the state record, it was a new junior college national record.

JACKIE ROBINSON

The record had been formerly held by none other than Mack Robinson, Jackie's older brother.

But this amazing athlete's day was not finished. As soon as he jumped his last jump, Jackie and his friends ran back to their car and headed for Glendale, California. Pasadena Junior College was playing Glendale for the state junior college baseball championship that day. Jackie arrived mid-game and promptly belted two hits and stole a base, helping his team to win. In one day, Jackie had broken a national record in track and helped his baseball team win a state championship with no practice jumps, no warm-ups, no batting practice or soft tossing—with nothing but incredible athletic talent, and a champion's heart.

As gifted as Jackie was in track, baseball and basketball, football might have been his best sport at Pasadena Junior College. Early in his first year, Jackie broke his ankle in practice. But when he

Jackie Stole a Base.

returned, he was named first-string quarterback and the team promptly won five straight games. The following year Pasadena won all eleven of its games.

Jackie not only played quarterback and running back, he used his dazzling speed and moves to return kickoffs and punts. Against Compton Junior College one day, he took a kickoff and seemed to have nowhere to go. Then something truly remarkable happened. A young man named Edwin Snider, watching in the stands, remembered, "He reversed his field three times and returned it for a touchdown. It was as dazzling a piece of broken-field running as you could ever hope to see."

Edwin—later known as Duke—would one day become a teammate of Jackie's on the Brooklyn Dodgers.

But it wasn't all easy for Jackie off and on the field during the years at Pasadena. When Jackie got to the college, he and two others were the only black players on the team; the white players, especially those that came from the South, refused to play with them. It got so bad that the first practice had to be canceled. But Jackie persevered.

Although he never became friends with any of his white teammates, both sides knew that the team would be stronger if they played together rather than fought each other. Jackie was instrumental in getting them to work together as a team. Though he fought bitterly against racism and prejudice wherever he saw it, Jackie always tried to build bridges between people.

But life was not easy for a black teenager in Pasadena, even if you were a four-letter star at the local junior college. One night when he and his friends were driving, a white motorist passed them and yelled racial taunts. Jackie and his friends exchanged words with the motorist and both cars

Jackie Was Arrested.

pulled over. Soon a fight broke out, with Jackie leading the way. The police became involved and Jackie was arrested for blocking a street and resisting arrest.

At the suggestion of his college advisors, Jackie agreed to pay a small fine and was assured the incident would be dropped from his records. Although Jackie felt he was innocent, he agreed because he had larger goals in mind.

Jackie was about to enroll at UCLA and have a chance to compete with other top athletes on the college level.

Chapter Four

U.C.L.A.

"Come to play for us, and we'll see you get everything you want," the man was saying to Jackie, on the front porch of the house on Pepper Street. Jackie and his brother Frank were sitting in two rickety chairs as the mosquitoes were just starting to come out in the early evening. "You want some cash in your pockets? To meet pretty girls? Nice clothes? We could get them for you. You want a brand new set of wheels? It's yours."

The man lifted a set of car keys out of his

"Come Play for Us."

pocket, jingled them in his hand and set them down on the table next to Jackie. "Think about it, kid!" he said as he left.

After he was gone, Jackie turned to Frank. "Sounds good to me!" he joked.

"Be serious, Jackie," Frank replied. Frank was Jackie's unofficial agent, helping him sift through all the offers from the four-year colleges after Jackie's magical two years at Pasadena.

"You have a lot of good offers to consider," Frank continued. "Washington and Washington State both want you. And UCLA and USC right in California. I think UCLA would be best, but you must decide for yourself."

"Thanks for helping me out with all this stuff," Jackie said, looking at Frank, and growing suddenly serious. Frank waved him off, as if to say it was nothing. The two brothers had grown even closer. Jackie was bigger and taller than Frank, but he still looked up to him.

Though married now, with two children of his own, Frank was still Jackie's biggest fan. He scouted opposing players and was always analyzing the strengths and weaknesses of Jackie's skills. Jackie admired his older brother's intelligence and loyalty.

"If I stay at home, I can see you and Mom every day," Jackie said.

"Whatever happens, I'll be there for you, little brother," Frank said, smiling. He got up and stepped down from the porch to his motorcycle, jumped on and rode off.

A few nights later, Jackie was at a neighbor's house, playing cards, when the phone rang.

It was Carl Anderson. "Jackie, Frank's been in a bad accident. You got to get to the hospital right away."

Jackie raced to the hospital as fast as he could.

He Saw Mallie in Shock.

JACKIE ROBINSON

When he reached Frank's room, he saw Mallie sitting there in shock. Frank was crying out in terrible pain. Jackie knew that his brother wasn't going to survive.

He couldn't stand seeing and hearing Frank in that kind of pain. Tears ran down his face as he raced back toward his house. He pulled a pillow over his head, trying to muffle the sound of Frank's cries echoing in his mind.

The next day Jackie sat in the kitchen with his mother. Frank had died early in the morning. Jackie watched silent tears roll down Mallie's face. It hurt him to see this strong, proud woman, who had raised her children singlehandedly with pride and courage, reduced to tears. Jackie put his arm around his mother and they cried together.

Knowing his mother would need him, as would Frank's widow and two young children, Jackie made the decision about college. He would stay close to home and go to the college Frank had wanted him to attend, UCLA.

At UCLA, for the first time, Jackie was not *the* star of his team. That role belonged to Kenny Washington, a senior and gifted tailback. Washington, known for his sunny and open disposition, was popular with his teammates as well.

Jackie was shy and withdrawn. He no longer had Frank to advise him, and the social transition to UCLA was not easy for him. But the football field was something different. Though Jackie often served as a decoy for Washington, drawing defenses toward him, Jackie's arrival clearly helped the team.

Against Stanford, Jackie had a 52-yard run from scrimmage and a 51-yard interception return in the same game. He ran for a total of 519 yards that season. But this number is deceptive, since Washington was the focus of the team. Jackie's

Jackie Was *Not* the Star.

impact as a player can be seen better from his amazing average gain from scrimmage, which was 11.28
yards per carry.

He continued his success on the basketball
court as well. Basketball was a game of timing and
precision passes in those days. Players didn't dunk
the ball, nor was the pace of the game as fast as it
is today. Jackie was known for his good shooting and
accurate passes. He vied with Ralph Vaughn from
USC for conference scoring honors that season.

In the last game of the season, with UCLA holding a slight lead over Stanford, Jackie held on to the
ball rather than shooting it, insuring his team's victory even though it meant losing the conference-
scoring title. Jackie Robinson was always a team
player. He was always ready to sacrifice his individual records for a team victory. It was winning, and
the team, that mattered most to him.

In outdoor track, he won broad-jump titles in

national meets and set more records. Jackie continued to play on the baseball diamond as well. Although baseball is the sport where Jackie made his name in later years, it was his weakest sport at college. If people at that time had been told that Jackie Robinson was going to be a famous baseball player, they would have been astonished!

Kenny Washington graduated after Jackie's first year and in his second year at UCLA, Jackie became the star of the football team. But this was a much weaker team than the last year's, and the team itself accomplished little.

Jackie, however, had a dominant year. Running and passing, he singlehandedly kept the team competitive in many games. Still, the Bruins won only one game that year, much to Jackie's disappointment.

The basketball team was also a weaker one that year. UCLA won only two of twelve conference

"I'm Rachel."

games, including an embarrassing 52–37 defeat to crosstown rival USC. Jackie, however, despite the team's weakness, was the PCC Southern Division scoring leader, averaging more than eleven points per game.

Though the performance of his teams was a disappointment, something else happened that would change his life.

"Jackie, you're the *man* on campus. Everyone knows you. I'm sure that little freshman would love to meet you," Ray Bartlee, Jackie's friend, told him one night at the student center.

"I'm not good at talking to girls like you are, Ray. Come on, help me out," Jackie answered.

Ray sauntered over to Rachel Isum, the girl who had caught Jackie's eye.

"Hi, I'm Ray," he introduced himself.

"I'm Rachel Isum," she answered in a clear strong voice.

JACKIE ROBINSON

"I got this friend, Rachel, who really wants to meet you. Can I bring you over and introduce him? His name is Jackie Robinson. He —"

"I know who Jackie Robinson is," Rachel interrupted him. "But why does Mr. Robinson need his friend to make his introductions for him? Does he think he's too important to come over himself, just because he's a big athletic star on campus?"

Ray laughed. This girl—pretty, intelligent, direct and unafraid to express her opinions—would be an interesting match for his shy, introverted friend.

"Rachel, Jackie's not at all like you think he is. He's a nice fellow, actually kind of shy."

"Nice fellow. I see how he stands around the backfield with his head cocked and his hands on his hips. Your friend is conceited and stuck on himself."

She turned and looked across the room to where Jackie was standing, looking hopefully toward her and Ray. Suddenly Rachel felt a blush coming over

Jackie Was Looking Toward Her.

her. Maybe she was wrong about Jackie—and after all, most girls would be delighted to have the attention of the big athlete on campus.

"Let's go over and meet this friend of yours," she said to Ray.

After Ray introduced Rachel to Jackie, he walked away wondering if the two of them would get along.

Right away, Jackie found Rachel easy to talk to. He told her about his family, his brother Mack, how he cared for his mother, and how he missed Frank.

Rachel told him about herself, how her mother was also a domestic like Mallie, how her father was ill and unable to work, and how she planned to become a nurse.

Jackie walked her to the parking lot, knowing he had met someone special but little realizing he was having his first conversation with his future wife.

Jackie's friendship with Rachel made his life on campus a lot happier. She helped him to open up more with people, so they wouldn't mistake his shyness for being conceited or defiant. But Jackie was unhappy at UCLA and decided to leave before he could graduate.

Mallie and Pastor Downs pleaded with Jackie to stay and finish his education. But Jackie felt strongly that it was time for him to leave. The Great Depression was not over yet. Job opportunities were scarce. Jackie realistically felt that there would be few good opportunities for a college–educated black man, and that whatever future he had lay in the field of coaching, where a college degree was not necessary at that time.

He also felt tired of living in what he called a "dream world." On campus he was a hero because of his athletic skills, but outside of UCLA, he was just another young black man in a society that offered little hope or opportunity. While Mallie and Karl Downs tried to convince him otherwise, only Rachel

UCLA's Greatest All-Around Athlete

supported his decision.

Jackie Robinson was the greatest all-around athlete in the history of UCLA. Today, an athlete of his skill, regardless of color, has tremendous financial and professional athletic opportunities waiting for him—product endorsements, big contracts, and millions of dollars.

But for Jackie Robinson, at that time, there were few opportunities. No job offers were waiting for him. None of the professional ball clubs would accept him because of the color of his skin.

It was Jackie Robinson, more than any other man, who brought about the opportunities black athletes have today.

Chapter 5

What To Do?

Jackie found a position as assistant athletic director at a national youth camp located between Los Angeles and San Francisco. It was the first time that Jackie lived away from home. There he was to play shortstop for the camp team, which battled other camps and local semipro teams for entertainment purposes.

He also worked with the youngsters at the camp, who came from poor and broken homes. He enjoyed working with these children and playing

He Worked with Youngsters at the Camp.

ball, but the camp was funded by a federal program that was soon canceled.

Jackie was looking around for a job when he received an offer for a three-week, all expenses paid trip to Chicago, where someone was organizing a game between college all-star football players and the Chicago Bears, of the National Football League. The Bears won the game easily, but Jackie played well even against professional competition.

He caught the eye of the owner of the Honolulu Bears, a semi-pro football team based in Hawaii. They offered Jackie a hundred dollars per game to play for the team and a construction job as well. Jackie and his friend Ray Bartlett accepted their offers.

It was difficult for Jackie to be so far away from his mother and from Rachel, who had become his steady girlfriend. But it would be for only two months, and Jackie needed the job, so he left for Hawaii in September 1941.

Jackie and Ray shared an apartment and did their construction work during the day. The Bears played and practiced at night because it was so hot in Hawaii. Ray was interested in construction and decided to stay after the season was over in November. But Jackie was missing his mother and Rachel and set sail back to California on December 5.

Two days later, on board ship Jackie was playing cards when he and the other fellows noticed the sailors painting the ship windows black. Suddenly the captain called all the passengers together to tell them some serious news. The Japanese had bombed Pearl Harbor, the American naval base in Hawaii, that morning, December 7. The United States was entering World War II.

When he returned, Jackie joined a semipro bas-

He Would Soon Be in the Army.

ketball team, the Los Angeles Red Devils. But Jackie knew this was only temporary, that he would soon be in the army.

History was making the calls now, not individuals or teams. Many men had to put their plans, and their lives, on hold.

Chapter 6

The Army Years

Jackie Robinson was inducted into the United States Army on March 23, 1942. He would serve for three years. After his physical he was posted in May of 1942 to Fort Riley, Kansas, where he completed basic training. Jackie applied to Officers' Candidate School (OCS) and passed the exam with high marks. But he and other young black men who also scored well on the test were turned down with no explanation.

The United States Army during World War II

With No Explanation

was completely segregated. Black soldiers could not serve in the same units as white soldiers, could not eat in the same mess halls, room in the same barracks, or even use the same latrines. Though these brave men were asked to be ready to sacrifice their lives for their country, they were not treated with dignity or respect.

As Jackie was walking through base one afternoon, angry and disappointed over his OCS rejection, he heard other black soldiers shouting and pointing. "It's the champ! It's the champ!" they called out.

Jackie looked up and saw a familiar face—Joe Louis, the great boxer and current heavyweight champion of the world. Louis, also serving in the army, had just been transferred to Fort Riley. He shook hands with many of the admiring young men, who saw Louis's achievement in the ring as proof that blacks could compete with whites on an equal basis, if given the chance. Jackie thought to introduce himself, but always on the shy side, decided not to bother the champ.

A few days later, Joe Louis walked over to a surprised Jackie.

"You're Jackie Robinson. I read a lot about you in the papers. You're quite an athlete, I hear. How about some golf?"

Jackie was flattered that Joe Louis had heard of him. Never shy when it came to pointing out injustice, he decided to use the opportunity to explain to Louis what had been happening to him and others regarding OCS.

During their golf games, Louis heard about Jackie's problems and immediately reacted. He called a contact in the Secretary of War's office in Washington, who flew out to meet with Louis and the young black soldiers and change the situation.

Jackie and his friends were admitted to OCS,

Jackie Wrote Many Letters to Rachel.

and in January, 1943, Jackie was commissioned as a second lieutenant. Jackie wrote many letters to Rachel, who was living in San Francisco at this time and studying nursing. He had sent her a bracelet and a ring, and the couple had announced their engagement. They planned to marry after Rachel graduated.

But the distance between them started to drive them apart. Rachel, too, began to think of joining the army as a cadet, and wrote to Jackie about it. When Jackie got her letter he grew jealous and angry.

"I don't want her on an army base surrounded by men," he told a friend. "If she joins, she can forget about us as a couple—we're through." Jackie's friends warned him not to give a proud and principled young woman like Rachel Isum that kind of ultimatum, but Jackie would not listen. Sure enough, Rachel was furious when she got Jackie's letter and mailed him back his bracelet and ring. Jackie knew he had made a mistake, but was too proud to admit it.

He tried to date other girls, but this didn't make him happy. There was a special magic between Jackie and Rachel, and Jackie knew that his pride and anger had gotten in the way.

Jackie was named morale officer for a unit of black soldiers. This was a difficult job, since morale was naturally low for soldiers who were the victims of institutional prejudice on a daily basis. Still, Jackie hoped to prove to his men that he could make a difference.

One especially upsetting rule for the soldiers was that they were forced to line up and wait for the few seats in the post exchange or canteen that were reserved for blacks, while the white section had an enormous number of seats available at all times.

Jackie called the provost officer on the tele-

Jackie Was Named Morale Officer.

phone to complain. The provost officer, not realizing that Jackie was black, used racial slurs and offensive language to explain the regulation. Jackie couldn't believe his ears. He felt his self-control slip away. He began to shout at the top of his voice over the phone. All the clerks at headquarters froze. Jackie's shouting was in earshot of Colonel Longley, his commanding officer.

The colonel quickly called Jackie into his office and demanded an explanation for his abusive language. Jackie complained to the colonel not only about the unfairness of the canteen situation but about the provost as well. To Jackie's surprise, Colonel Longley listened with great sympathy and promised to write a letter to higher-ups about both the canteen and the racist language used by the provost officer.

Although separate black and white canteen sections remained in place, more seats were added for blacks. Jackie felt grateful to Colonel Longley, who had taken a stand against injustice and he was glad to show the men in his unit that change could take place if people spoke out.

Jackie, who had spent most of his earliest years on the playing field, missed competitive sports when he was in the army. There was lots of athletic competition taking place, as many college and professional athletes had been drafted or volunteered for the army during World War II. But the army was segregated and this situation created difficulties.

Early in the spring of 1943, Jackie had wandered over to Fort Riley's baseball field where some soldiers were playing. When he asked to join the game, Jackie was turned down. Two of the white soldiers playing ball that day were Dixie Walker and Pete Reiser, who would someday be Jackie's teammates on the Brooklyn Dodgers.

Reiser, years later, wrote, "I didn't know who he

He Appealed to Jackie to Play.

was then, but that was the first time I saw Jackie Robinson. I can still remember him walking away by himself."

A colonel in charge of the base football team, however, wanted Jackie to play because he knew how good Jackie was. He personally appealed to Jackie to play, but told him that against certain teams he would have to sit out, because they would refuse to play against an African American.

Jackie said he would consider it and asked for a two-week furlough to visit his family. Jackie knew he would not play under those conditions; he said he would consider it just so he could get his furlough.

Back at home in Pasadena, Jackie greeted his mother and played with his brother Frank's children. But Mallie noticed that her usually cheerful son was looking gloomy and sad.

"Jackie, I know why you're just moping around. You're missing Rachel. Why don't you just take that old car of yours and ride up to San Francisco and make up?"

"But Mama, she sent me back my ring, she—"

"Hush up, son," Mallie interrupted. "Never let false pride get in your way. You know you care about that girl. And she's a fine girl. You're never going to do better than Rachel Isum. You know you want her back, so give her a call."

Jackie telephoned Rachel, who sounded happy to hear from him. She had been missing him as much as he had been missing her.

A few minutes later Jackie bounded down the stairs, his duffle bag under his arm. "Going to see Rachel, Mama!" he called out as he raced toward his car. Then he turned back and gave his mother a kiss. "Mama, you know everything. Thanks."

Mallie Robinson watched her son sprint down the street, fire up his car and speed away. *That boy is always running,* she said to herself, *but he's run-*

"Going to See Rachel, Mama!"

ning in the right direction.

Jackie could have set a new speed record with his drive ride up to San Francisco! After a few awkward moments, he and Rachel were a couple once more. Jackie spent every hour he could with her. Because he couldn't afford a hotel, he slept in his car. But it was worth it. He knew now, that after the war was over, he and Rachel would be together forever.

When Jackie returned to Fort Riley, he told the colonel he would not play football for him. His decision, as well as his steady refusal to be silent in the face of unfair regulations for blacks, had not made Jackie too popular with many higher-ups at the base. Soon after his return he was transferred to Fort Hood, Texas.

Chapter 7

Court-martialed

At Fort Hood, Jackie was assigned to the 761st Tank Battalion under the command of Colonel Paul L. Bates. Colonel Bates, who was white, was considered a tough but fair commander.

The battalion he whipped into shape became a brave and successful fighting unit. It served under General Patton overseas and proved itself with great courage.

Jackie was a platoon leader of the B company of the 761st Batallion. When he arrived he told the

They Outperformed the White Units.

men under him that he knew next to nothing about tanks and they would have to teach him. His men responded well to his honesty, and the unit trained brilliantly. Under Colonel Bates's directions, they outperformed the white units on the base and were poised to fight overseas.

Jackie Robinson had been admitted to the army on a limited service basis due to the ankle injury he had suffered in college. In order to fight overseas, he would have to be re-examined by an army doctor and sign a waiver relieving the army of responsibility should his ankle sustain further damage.

On Colonel Bates's advice, Jackie went to have his ankle checked by the base doctor. After a long wait without being examined, Jackie returned to the base. Finding his men on maneuvers, he decided to return to the hospital. He noticed the wife of a fellow black officer on the bus and sat down next to her.

JACKIE ROBINSON

Army buses were often segregated in those days, especially in the South. Black soldiers were forced to sit in the back of the bus, and had to get off if the bus were crowded and no seats were available. But at that time things had also begun to change. Jackie knew that recently Joe Louis and Sugar Ray Robinson had refused to move to the back of an army bus, which had caused the army to put through regulations barring discrimination by race on any army vehicle.

But this regulation had not been enforced in Texas, and the bus driver, seeing Jackie in the middle of the bus, grew angry. He seemed especially angry because the woman Jackie was sitting next to was a light-skinned black, whom the bus driver mistakenly thought was white. He stopped the bus and went to Jackie, telling him to move to the back.

When the bus driver returned to the seat he was surprised to see that Jackie had refused to

The Bus Driver Grew Angry.

move. When he saw Jackie still in his seat he began to shout at him. Jackie would not back down and the driver continued his route, warning Jackie there would be trouble.

The bus driver radioed his dispatcher for help and when Jackie got off the bus at the last stop, a jeep filled with military police screeched to a halt in front of him. Since Jackie was a superior officer, they treated him with courtesy and asked him to accompany them to see the duty officer. Jackie agreed to go. He was outraged by the bus driver's offensive language. He knew he had not been in any violation of army regulations, so he assumed he could straighten things out.

The duty officer and his secretary began questioning Jackie in a rude and offensive way. Jackie felt his anger grow and answered them back in kind.

The duty officer, a Captain Bear, called Jackie "uppity" and reminded him of his "place." Jackie

Robinson would have none of that. He accused the captain of racism and demanded a fair hearing. Soon a colonel was called in and there was talk of a court-martial.

The colonel had been told there was a drunk and disorderly black officer causing trouble. When he saw a very angry but very sober Jackie Robinson, he immediately told Jackie to ask for a blood test to prove that he had not been drinking alcohol. This was the South, where the truth was not sufficient defense for a black man.

Jackie was released to Colonel Bates. Colonel Bates suggested he take a short leave, and he would try to resolve the incident so Jackie could go overseas with his unit.

Back in California, Jackie visited Rachel. Rachel was not in the best of spirits herself. Her brother had been shot down overseas and was presumed dead. She had begun to think again of join-

He Would Have to Face a Court-Martial.

ing the army. Jackie was again jealous at the thought of Rachel serving on an army base. They started to argue.

But Jackie would not make the same mistake twice. He met Rachel every night after she finished work. He grieved with her over her missing brother and rejoiced with her when he was found alive. She sympathized with him over his difficulties back in Texas, and they emerged from this rough period more attached than ever.

When Jackie returned to Fort Hood, he received bad news. He would have to face a court-martial. Colonel Bates refused to sign a court-martial order, but other officers did.

Court-martials most often find against the defendants, but Jackie felt he had right on his side. Fellow black officers had begun to write letters on his behalf. The black press began to report the incident and the army began to feel pressure about prosecuting a former college athletic star, just because he had refused to move to the back of a bus.

Jackie's army attorney was a brilliant young man from Michigan who exposed the inconsistencies and lies in the prosecution's testimonies. The case was an obvious frame-up and all charges were dismissed.

But Jackie's army career was definitely over. He wrote to the Adjutant General's office in Washington, asking for a discharge. Jackie Robinson was fed up with the army and the army was glad to have him go, considering him a troublemaker for standing up for his rights. In November of 1944, Jackie received his honorable discharge.

All Charges Were Dismissed.

Chapter 8

The Negro Leagues

When Jackie Robinson was discharged from the army, he had the ability to excel on any professional team in the country in three sports; football, basketball, and baseball.

But such a career was denied to him, as all professional team sports were closed to African Americans. So at the age of twenty-five, Jackie had few prospects. He had to help out his mother and Frank's family. He also wanted to start earning money so he could marry Rachel. But what was he to do?

Temporary help came in the form of an offer to coach the men's basketball season for the fall and winter of 1944 at Sam Houston College in Texas. The offer was arranged through Jackie's old friend, Karl Downs. Tiny Sam Houston College was an all-black school with only thirty-five male students. Still, Jackie's hard work and competitive drive helped him lead the school to a winning record. But after the season was over, Jackie needed money and a new job.

When he was in the army, he had heard that the Kansas City Monarchs baseball team was looking for players and paid them decent money. The Monarchs were a team in the Negro Leagues. Since the 1880s, blacks, who were not allowed to play in the major leagues, had formed their own leagues.

Negro league teams often played in the same ballparks as the major leaguers, but only when the

Their Games Were Well Attended.

major league franchises were out of town. They had strong followings in the black community, and their games were well attended. Crowds averaged about 10,000 people per game, and All-Star games saw as many as 50,000 fans attending.

During the major-league off-season, white stars often played barnstorming games against Negro League teams and were aware of the talent of the black ballplayers. All the records and history of baseball would today be different, if some of these great black players had been allowed in the majors.

Earlier, black stars such as John Henry Lloyd played in barnstorming games against Hall of Famers like Honus Wagner and Babe Ruth. Ruth was amazed at Lloyd's talent, and Wagner thought he was the best player he had ever seen. John McGraw, the fiery manager of the New York Giants, deeply admired the talent in the Negro Leagues and campaigned to have black players admitted to the majors. But the commissioner of baseball, Judge Kenesaw Mountain Landis, as well as most of the team owners, was against it.

Today the exploits of all-time great pitchers, like Christy Mathewson, are still celebrated. But what is little known is that Mathewson won only 14 games as a rookie pitcher. The following spring, McGraw had Charlie Grant, a pitcher from the Negro Leagues, teach him the screwball in spring training. Mathewson went on to win 34 games that year and to dominate the sport, eventually earning his way to the Hall of Fame. Grant never pitched even a single inning in the major leagues.

When Ted Williams was inducted into the Hall of Fame, he stated that the Hall of Fame would not represent the true history of baseball until it honored the great black ballplayers who played in the Negro Leagues and were kept out of the majors. Happily, the trustees of the Hall of Fame listened to

But the Commissioner Was Against It.

Williams's words, and today, stars of the Negro Leagues are honored at the Hall of Fame in Cooperstown, New York.

The management of the Monarchs wrote to Jackie Robinson, offering him a tryout at their spring training camp in Houston with a salary of $400 a week, minus expenses and meal money, should he make the team. Playing professional baseball meant long hours on the road and little chance to see Rachel. But Jackie needed the money, so he accepted the offer.

Professional ballplayers in the major leagues in the 1940s did not receive the huge salaries they do today. But they lived very good lives. Teams traveled in top-of-the-line buses or first-class railway compartments. They stayed in good hotels and ate in top restaurants. They were celebrities, welcomed wherever they went.

Not so for the players in the Negro Leagues. They had to play as many as four games in one day. They would travel long hours in old buses that frequently broke down. They often slept in the buses as most hotels would not accept black people. They often ate their meals in the buses as they were not welcomed in restaurants. The only things that kept them going were their monthly paychecks and their love for the game.

When Jackie joined the Monarchs in 1945, they were already an elite team in the Negro Leagues, with stars like Satchel Paige, Hilton Smith, and Othello Renfroe. They competed against teams that included older, established Negro League stars like Josh Gibson, Buck Leonard, and Cool Papa Bell.

Bell, Gibson, and Paige would undoubtedly have been dominating players had they been permitted to play in the major leagues at that time. Satchel Paige had an amazing variety of pitches

Satchel Paige Was a Great Showman.

that he could throw for strikes. He was a great show-man who delighted in showing up the opposition. (Paige eventually did play in the major leagues, but he was long past his prime at that point.)

Gibson hit 75 home runs one year. He is cred-ited with having hit the longest home run in Yankee Stadium, during a Negro League game. It is very possible that Gibson would have put up statistics to match Babe Ruth's had he been allowed to play in the majors.

But it was Cool Papa Bell whose play most influenced Jackie Robinson. Bell was a slashing, daring base runner who could drive pitchers to dis-traction. He would take a giant lead off first base, tantalizing the pitcher into throwing over. But when he took off for second, he didn't show that big lead. He just used his incredible quickness.

Bell dominated games not only at the plate, but on the base paths. When Jackie reached the major leagues he would do much the same. Today's baseball, with its emphasis on speed and picking up the extra base, was influenced by Jackie Robinson's style of play. But few people know that Jackie had learned much of this style from watching Cool Papa Bell.

Jackie did well in his season with the Monarchs. He hit about .350 and played an adequate shortstop. But it was not a happy time for him. He missed Rachel. He objected to the difficult conditions the players lived under, and he did not feel all that comfortable with the other players. Jackie was one of the few college-educated players in the Negro Leagues. He had been a star at a largely white university and did not feel at home in a league where many of the players accepted the substandard conditions of their lives without rebelling.

The cost for not rebelling was high. Many of the frustrated players in the Negro Leagues drank alco-

He Hit about .350.

hol to excess and did not keep themselves in good condition. Jackie neither drank nor smoked, and tried to keep himself in shape. But he was angered by having to accept the limitations segregation placed on him. He felt like exploding.

On a particularly hot Alabama summer day, the team bus pulled up at a filling station. Jackie got off the bus to go to the bathroom.

"Where's the bathroom?" he asked the young gas station attendant.

"Your bathroom's over that way," the young man answered, gesturing. Jackie noticed a bathroom a few feet away and headed toward it.

"That bathroom's not for coloreds, boy!"

Jackie ignored these words and used the whites only bathroom. When he came out, the attendant started yelling and swearing at him. Instinctively Jackie pulled back and punched him.

"Get in, get in quick!" called the other players.

JACKIE ROBINSON

The team manager left the money on the gas pump with the attendant unconscious and draped over the hose.

On board, the players gathered around Jackie. They reminded him of where he was—Alabama—where black people could be lynched for behavior like that.

Jackie tried to calm himself. But deep inside he knew life in the Negro Leagues was not for him. He had too much trouble accepting racial injustice without fighting back. He felt as if he were all alone in this fight—that even the other black players had lost the will or energy to struggle.

What Jackie did not know then was that there was a man in this country who also wanted to see black players play alongside white players with respect and dignity; a man who had the position, the ability, and the courage to make that dream possible. His name was Branch Rickey.

Two Heroes

Chapter 9

Branch Rickey

There are two heroes in the Jackie Robinson story. There is Jackie Robinson himself, the courageous young black man who endured and suffered threats and intimidation from those inside and outside of baseball, overcame them all, and triumphed.

There is also the more surprising hero, Branch Rickey—the general manager of the Brooklyn Dodgers, an older man, white, politically and socially conservative, deeply religious, known for his skill in evaluating and putting together talent on a baseball field, Rickey didn't hesitate to risk his reputation, his standing in the baseball community, and the chemistry of his very successful team to do what he thought was right.

The Jackie Robinson story is also very much the story of Branch Rickey.

Branch Rickey was a baseball man. As a young man he had served as the baseball coach at his alma mater, Ohio Wesleyan University. Afterward he had gone on to play at the professional level, as both a minor leaguer and major leaguer. He reached the major leagues in 1906 as a catcher for the St. Louis Browns. After he made it with the Browns, he married his childhood sweetheart, Jane. Then in the winter of 1907 he was traded to the New York Yankees.

Rickey looked like a catcher, burly with thick legs and large hands. He was known for his enormous strength and stamina. As he went into spring

Rickey Looked Like a Catcher.

training in 1907, newly and happily married, playing in New York and in top shape, the whole world
seemed to be before him.

But as the season wore on, Rickey knew something was wrong. He grew increasingly weak and
was constantly getting colds and coughing spells.
Branch Rickey had tuberculosis, a disease that was
often fatal. He had to spend a year at a sanitarium
in upstate New York. When he was released, he was
told that his playing days were over.

Rickey did not despair. He was a deeply religious man. Throughout his career in baseball, he
refused to play or attend games on Sundays. His
faith helped him through this difficult period, and
he decided to go to law school.

Rickey attended law school at the University of
Michigan, and after graduation set up a law practice
in Montana. But Rickey found himself missing the
game he loved. In 1913, he was back in baseball as

the manager of the St. Louis Browns. He moved over to the St. Louis Cardinals in 1917, where he served as manager and general manager in charge of the overall development of the team.

The Cardinals' owner, Sam Breadon, did not like Rickey's style of managing. He replaced him as manager in 1925 with Rogers Hornsby, keeping Rickey as general manager. In 1926, Rickey and Hornsby led the Cardinals to a World Series victory over the New York Yankees and Babe Ruth.

This was a tremendous achievement, as the Cardinals had assembled a team in what was then a completely new way.

The great teams of the past had been assembled through trades and purchases of already established players. Wealthier teams often purchased the contracts of great players from teams that were in poorer financial shape. The wealthy New York Yankees, for instance, had purchased Babe Ruth, prob-

He Built the Farm System.

ably the greatest player in the history of baseball, from the Boston Red Sox. Many of the other Yankee greats from this era had also come from trades and purchases.

When Branch Rickey took over the Cardinals, they did not even have the money to go to Florida for spring training. Rickey decided he would have to build a team with younger players. He hired scouts to search for talented players all over the country. His scouts would sign these young players; then Rickey would make arrangements with minor league teams to give them playing time.

Rickey would use the minor leagues as a training ground. When the young players had refined their skills he would bring them up to the Cardinals. He built what he called a "farm system."

Rickey's idea worked brilliantly. His farm system enabled him to replace aging players with young talent and keep building for the future as well. Soon other teams, like the Cincinnati Reds and the New York Yankees, developed their own farm systems.

Eventually, the farm system was adopted and formalized by every professional baseball team. Branch Rickey had changed the structure of baseball.

Rickey had many successful years with the Cardinals. But he and Sam Breadon never got along very well. After the fall of 1942, a year in which the Cardinals had again won the World Series, Breadon refused to renew Rickey's contract. In 1943, the Dodgers of Brooklyn, New York were in need of a new general manager, so Rickey moved on.

By 1945, after two years on the job, Rickey had begun to assemble the kind of team he liked. He knew that the Dodgers had many established players who had been serving in the armed forces during World War II. He had decided to spend his first few years, as he had done at St. Louis, building for

Rickey Moved On.

the future.

This decision had won Rickey few friends in New York. The press and fans always expect an instant winner. Rickey had also replaced the very popular Larry McPhail as general manager of the Dodgers. McPhail was colorful and flamboyant. Rickey was religious, did not drink alcohol and was not a free spender.

But Branch Rickey was about to do something that would be far more controversial than anything else he had done in his whole career. By 1945 he had decided to break an unwritten code—the code that baseball teams should be all-white. It was a decision that would not only change the history of baseball, but would change America as well.

In March, 1945, Branch Rickey invited the Dodgers' radio announcer, Red Barber, to lunch. Barber had grown up in the South. As the "voice" of the Dodgers and a Southerner, Barber could be instrumental in a black player's acceptance by the fans. Rickey decided to tell Barber in advance about his plans to integrate the Dodgers.

"Red," he whispered over lunch that day, "I'm about to tell you something only the Dodgers' board of directors and my wife know. What I'm going to tell you is something you have to keep secret. You can only tell your wife."

Barber waited in suspense. Rickey was a masterful storyteller and Barber knew something important was about to be discussed.

"When I was a college coach at Ohio Wesleyan in 1904," Rickey went on, "I took my team down to South Bend, Indiana to play Notre Dame. When I came to the hotel to register my players, the hotel clerk refused to register one of them. That was a fine young man named Charley Thomas, and the only reason they would not let him in was because of the color of his skin.

"I'm Going to Do Something About It."

JACKIE ROBINSON

"I convinced the clerk to let Charley stay in my room without formally registering, and I sent him up to our room while I waited for the rest of the team to register.

"When I got up to our room, Charley was sitting on the edge of a chair. He was crying and pulling at the skin on his hands, as if he wanted to peel it off.

'It's my skin, Mr. Rickey, it's my skin. If I could pull it off, I'd be just like everybody else.' That was forty-one years ago, and for forty-one years I have heard that young man's words in my head. And now I'm going to do something about it."

Barber sat back stunned. He had expected dramatic news, but nothing like this. He sat in shock as Rickey continued.

"I am 64 years old. My wife and children tell me I'm not up to it, that I've gone through enough, that all of baseball may be against me. But I'm going to do it. I'm going to sign a black player."

JACKIE ROBINSON

Red Barber had grown up in the South, prejudiced toward black people. If he resigned from his job in protest at Rickey's action, it would have created even further controversy. But Barber was struck by the sincerity and power of Rickey's words and decided to stay.

Rickey went on to spell out his plan to Barber. "I've told people I am developing an all-black team to play in Brooklyn when the Dodgers are out of town. That's why people think I've sent so many scouts to all the Negro league teams. But the scouts don't know they are really searching for the first black player I can put on the Dodgers. I don't know yet who or where this young man is, but I know one thing for sure. He *is* coming!"

"He *Is* Coming!"

Chapter 10

Signing Jackie

Rickey sent his scouts to gather as much information as they could about the players currently in the Negro Leagues. The number-one requirement was that the player Rickey ultimately chose would need the talent to play on a major league level.

There were many players, the scouts reported, with that kind of talent. Rickey also needed to choose a young player. He wanted someone who could develop and mature as a player, rather than an established Negro League star. This eliminated men like Satchel Paige and Cool Papa Bell, who were already in or past their prime.

Rickey received reports almost daily in his office in Brooklyn. The name that kept appearing was a hard-hitting, swift-running shortstop for the Kansas City Monarchs named Jackie Robinson.

Rickey sent his three top scouts to watch Robinson play—Wid Matthews, George Sisler and Clyde Sukeforth. The reports were all glowing about Robinson's baseball abilities, although some questioned whether he had a strong enough arm to play shortstop.

Branch Rickey knew, however, that talent wasn't the only requirement necessary for the first black ballplayer to play in the major leagues. That player would need intelligence, courage and a fierce will. He would also need the ability to bear verbal and even physical abuse without striking back. Would Jackie Robinson be the right man?

He Had to Look Even Deeper.

JACKIE ROBINSON

Once he received the reports from the scouts, Rickey decided to research Jackie's character. He liked that Jackie had attended college and was pleased to learn that like Rickey himself, Jackie was known for his clean lifestyle, abstaining from alcohol and late-night parties.

But signing Jackie to a major league contract was an historic decision, and Rickey decided he had to look even deeper.

Sources at UCLA told him that Jackie was a fantastic all-around athlete. But these sources also told Rickey that Jackie Robinson demanded equality and would not be demeaned due to the color of his skin. Jackie was described as a "racial agitator."

Rickey was concerned but not put off by this report. He wanted a man who was proud of his skin color. He knew that a person more accepting of racial intolerance might be beaten down by the reaction he would get. Rickey wanted someone with fierce determination and pride. And no one had more of that than Jackie Robinson.

The report from the army was more disturbing. Although Jackie was cleared during his court martial, the army implied he could not get along with white officers and had major problems with authority. There was only one thing to do, Rickey decided. He would meet Jackie face-to-face.

On a hot summer day in August, 1945, Jackie stood around the batting cage in Comiskey Park, Chicago. The Chicago White Sox of the major leagues were out of town, and the Kansas City Monarchs of the Negro Leagues had paid to use their facilities for practice. Rumors had gone around that a new Negro League team was being formed back East, so Jackie was not surprised when he heard that Clyde Sukeforth, a Dodgers' scout, had come to see him.

"I'd like to see you throw from the hole," Clyde

Jackie Was Not Surprised

told Jackie.

"My arm's sore. I'm not supposed to throw for a week or two," Jackie answered.

"That's okay," Sukeforth said. "Come meet me tonight. I want to talk to you."

Jackie was unimpressed. Negro League players did not expect much from the major leagues. Once, black players had been invited to try out at the Red Sox camp and Jackie had gone along. It was clear that the manager never took them seriously, and Jackie and his friends had left feeling they had wasted their time.

But Sukeforth seemed like a decent man. Jackie decided to talk to him. At the hotel, Sukeforth got down to business.

"Branch Rickey wants to start a team called the Brooklyn Brown Dodgers, and he is interested in you. He wants to meet you in New York. He'll pay for your ticket and the expenses."

Jackie shrugged. He had nothing to lose since he couldn't play with his arm injured anyway.

After a long train ride, Sukeforth brought him to the Dodgers' office in Brooklyn to meet with Rickey. For Rickey, Robinson already had two strikes against him, the reports from UCLA and the army. Jackie entered the meeting suspicious, a little angry and almost hostile. It was not a promising start.

After he introduced the two men, Sukeforth left. Jackie thought Branch Rickey was an impressive-looking man. He had a deep, booming voice and an air of command. He shook Jackie's hand vigorously. They both sat down.

"Do you have a girlfriend?" Rickey suddenly asked.

Jackie was surprised by the question. "I do ... at least I think I do," Jackie answered. He went on to explain how much he cared about Rachel, but how she had her nursing career, and how he was always

Not the Conversation He Expected

on the road. He told Rickey of his hopes and plans.

"I'm glad you have a girl," Rickey answered, "because there are times a man needs someone close to him by his side."

Jackie felt his heart start to race. The conversation was not going as he had expected.

"I don't know what this is about. Mr. Sukeforth told me that I was a candidate for the Brooklyn Brown Dodgers and..."

"That's what he was supposed to tell you," Rickey interrupted. "The truth is, Jackie, you are not a candidate for the Brooklyn Brown Dodgers. I wanted to see you because I am interested in you as a candidate for the Brooklyn Dodgers of the National League. I think you can play in the majors. What do you think?"

Jackie sat back. He was excited, scared, stunned. He could not say a word.

"You think you could play for Montreal, our

minor-league team?"

"Yes," Jackie said simply.

Rickey had done what he wanted. First he had put Jackie at ease with a smile and a handshake, then he had shaken him up. Now was the time to test him further.

He leaned forward in his chair. He ran his thick hand through his gray hair and almost jabbed at Jackie, gesturing with his unlit cigar.

"I know you're a good ballplayer, Jackie. My scouts have told me that. What I don't know is if you have the guts."

Jackie felt blood rushing to his cheeks. Here was a virtual stranger, questioning his courage, almost calling him a coward. He started to rise in anger.

From the other side of his desk, Rickey could sense Jackie's anger surge. He sensed the deep self-pride in the man—the combative, competitive nature. He told friends much later that he knew

"I Don't Know If You Have Guts."

immediately that Jackie was the most competitive person he had met since Ty Cobb. He knew he had to keep on going at him.

"Have you got the guts to play, no matter what happens? Because there is more at stake here than hits, runs and errors. A baseball box score is the most democratic thing in the world. It tells you what a man did that day..."

"But it's the box score that really counts," Jackie interrupted.

"It's all that *ought* to count. And with your help, young man, one day it may be. But right now you're going to need an awful lot of courage."

Jackie stared at Branch Rickey. He was impressed and moved by the sincerity and honesty in Rickey's words. He had never met anyone quite like this old man.

"Have you got the guts to play, no matter what?" Rickey asked again.

JACKIE ROBINSON

"I can play the game, Mr. Rickey," Jackie answered.

Rickey got up and moved around the other side of the desk.

"Well, this is what's going to happen," he continued. "White people all over America are going to see a black man play *against*, and even more importantly, *with* white men. And many of them are not going to like it. You are going to get letters filled with hate and fear. Some may even threaten you.

"At the ballpark you're going to hear people in the stands scream at you. Some are going to utter the worst racial slurs you ever heard. Your girlfriend will be in the stands hearing this stuff. When the team travels, some railroads and hotels won't let you in.

"Everyone else on the team will be together and you will have to be by yourself. Your own teammates may not accept you at first. You are going to be alone in the locker room. And other teams are going to say

"A Man Afraid to Fight Back?"

and do rough, rough things.

"You're going to get beanballs thrown at your head. They're going to call out curses from the dugout.

"When you slide into second base, someone may spike you, and when the blood is running down your leg, say, 'How you like that, boy?'

"Mr. Rickey, are you looking for a black man who is afraid to fight back?" Jackie asked.

"Robinson," Rickey almost shouted, "I'm looking for a ballplayer with the guts enough *not* to fight back. Because the only way for a black man to break the color line is not to retaliate. Not to answer a blow with a blow or a curse with a curse."

Jackie thought of the time when he was eight years old and threw rocks at the girl who had shouted racial insults at him. His whole life he had fought back, answering prejudice with his words or with his fists. Now Branch Rickey was asking him to do precisely the opposite.

"Three years, Mr. Robinson," Branch Rickey's voice had turned into a hoarse whisper. "Three years. That's what I'm asking from you.

"At the end of those three years, I give you my word you can say and do what you want. Because by the end of those three years, if you do what I say, there will be more and more black players in baseball. No one will be able to stop it. Three years, that's what I'm asking for. Can you do it?"

Jackie looked into Branch Rickey's eyes.

"Mr. Rickey, I've got to do it!"

They shook hands. An old man and a young man. A white man and a black man. In that handshake was a sign and a promise—a promise of a better future not only for baseball, but for America.

"I've Got to Do It!"

Chapter 11

Montreal

On October 23, 1945, the Montreal Royals—the minor-league affiliate of the Brooklyn Dodgers—called a press conference to announce the signing of Jack Roosevelt Robinson to a minor league contract. It was official. Jackie Robinson and Branch Rickey had broken the color line that had kept African Americans out of organized baseball.

Present at the press conference were Branch Rickey, Jr., who was in charge of the Brooklyn Dodgers farm system; Hector Racine, the president of the Montreal Royals; and Jackie Robinson. When interviewed, Jackie responded with pride and honesty. "Of course, I can't begin to tell you how happy I am that I am the first member of my race in organized ball. I realize how much it means to me, my race, and to baseball. I can only say I'll do my very best to come through in every manner."

Reactions to the signing were mixed. Some sportswriters criticized the Dodgers and Branch Rickey; others were supportive. Former and active baseball stars like Rogers Hornsby, Bob Feller, and Dixie Walker were openly critical. Many questioned Jackie's ability and claimed he would not have been signed had he been white.

Many Negro League players were angry and jealous that Robinson had been selected by the Dodgers as the first black player. After all, he had only played one year in the Negro Leagues while they had spent years toiling for little pay and less

A Special Burden

respect. But other Negro League players wished Jackie well. They knew he was taking on a special burden by being the first black player and wanted him to achieve success.

Jackie had earlier agreed to go to Venezuela that winter to play for a Negro League all-star team against various South American teams. Cool Papa Bell, that legend of the game, worked with Jackie on base running skills and defense. Gene Benson, of the Philadelphia Stars, spent hours with Jackie on defense and offering him instructions on how to hit the curve ball.

Jackie did not play especially well that winter. He was already starting to feel the pressure building. He was hearing the criticism in the white press and feeling the resentment of fellow Negro League players as well. This pressure was only sure to increase as the time came closer for him to join the Montreal Royals for spring training.

JACKIE ROBINSON

Writers for the black press were the ones who most understood the enormous pressure Jackie was under. Ludlow Werner, the editor of the *New York Age,* summed up Jackie's burden: "He will be haunted by the expectations of his race. To 15,000,000 Negroes he will symbolize not only their prowess in baseball, but their ability to rise to an opportunity. Unlike white players, he can never afford an off-day or an off-night. His private life will be watched, too, because white America will judge the Negro race by everything he does." This was indeed a heavy burden for one man to handle.

Jackie remembered Branch Rickey's advice at their meeting. He would need someone by his side to share his hopes and fears, to confide his doubts to, to share his triumphs with. Shortly after his return to the United States, on February 10, 1946, Jackie Robinson and Rachel Isum were married in Los Angeles. The Reverend Karl Downs flew in from

Jackie and Rachel Were Married.

Texas to officiate at the wedding.

After a brief honeymoon, Jackie and Rachel were off to Florida where the Royals had their spring training camp. But getting there wasn't easy. Jackie and Rachel were continually bumped from their seats at various stops in favor of white passengers.

Finally, when they reached Florida they were again removed from a plane at Pensacola and forced to take a bus to Jacksonville. They were made to sit in the black-only section at the back of the bus. Jackie seethed with anger and suffered for Rachel, who had never been subjected to this kind of treatment before.

The reception for Jackie at the Royals training camp was not a cheerful one. Most of the other Royals players ignored him. The Royals' manager, Clay Hopper, was from Mississippi, and though he was loyal to Branch Rickey, he had no wish for Jackie to be on his team. Jackie and Rachel lived separately from the rest of the team, as all the hotels were still segregated in the South.

Even worse was the reaction of the local fans and communities. The Royals were forced to move from Sanford to Daytona because the town of Sanford would not allow blacks and whites to play on the same ball field. A game against the Jersey City Giants in Jacksonville was cancelled because there was a local law forbidding blacks and whites to play together.

Fans would call out racial slurs and curse at Jackie. He would glance over in the stands, knowing Rachel had to hear all of this. It was hard to endure. To make matters worse, in an effort to win the starting shortstop job, Jackie had thrown too hard and injured his shoulder. His batting average started to dip, too.

"Maybe I'm not good enough to make it," he confided to Rachel.

"I Can't Stand the Way We're Treated."

JACKIE ROBINSON

"You're trying too hard," Rachel answered, rubbing his shoulder. "Mr. Rickey wants you on that team. Just the other day, he told you that if your arm wasn't strong enough for shortstop, you could play second."

"But it's more than that, Rachel. I can't stand the way we're treated down here. It hurts me to have you hearing all that stuff people yell out, as if I were some kind of animal, something less than human. It's not right for my wife to hear that stuff."

"Don't you worry about me, Jackie Robinson," Rachel said smiling. "Soon we'll be up north and things will be better."

Despite a relatively weak showing in training camp, Jackie went north as the Royals' starting second baseman. The season opened in Jersey City. A packed house of 51,000 jammed into a stadium that only had 25,000 seats to see Jackie's first regular season game. Thousands of black fans came out to root for Jackie. Shrewd baseball men took note that black ballplayers could be powerful drawing cards and bring even more financial gain to the owners.

Jackie felt great that day. During batting practice he felt the ball jumping off his bat. His legs felt fresh and his arm no longer hurt. He smacked a sharp single for his first minor-league hit.

In the top half of the third inning, the Giants' pitcher tried to sneak a fastball past him. Jackie drove the ball over 340 feet for his first home run as a pro. As he rounded the bases, he heard the crowd explode in cheers, even though he was playing for the opposing team. He smiled as he looked up at Rachel in the stands. But even more important was when his teammates came to congratulate him. For the first time, Jackie started to feel like part of the team.

He remembered what Branch Rickey had told him. His play on the field would be what would over-

His First Minor-League Hit

come his teammates' ignorance and prejudice. In his next at-bat, Jackie dropped a perfect bunt down the third baseline for a base hit. He studied the pitcher's motion, and when he got the sign, easily stole second base. An infield out moved him to third.

Now he stood on third base and recalled two special conversations. Branch Rickey had told him to be aggressive on the base paths— to use his speed to dominate a game. He also remembered what Cool Papa Bell had told him one day.

"When you get on third base, it's time to play with the pitcher's head. On one pitch you charge down the line like you're goin' to steal home and then you put the brakes on. You dance on those base paths. You intimidate, you confuse, you shake them up. That's how we play in the Negro leagues. When you play in the majors, you bring *our* game to them. You do that and you're sure to succeed."

Jackie bolted down the line, then ran back to

third, faking stealing home. He did it again. The Giants' pitcher became completely distracted until he balked, allowing Jackie to score from third. Aggression on the base paths—this was to become Jackie Robinson's trademark throughout his professional career.

It was early evening in Manhattan. Branch Rickey and some friends were about to have dinner in a restaurant, celebrating a Dodgers' victory in Brooklyn that day. Rickey had stayed away from Jersey City because he thought his presence might put even more pressure on Jackie. But he had sent an aide there to find out what happened.

As Rickey and his party were about to be seated, the aide rushed in with the results from Jersey City. "Mr. Rickey..." he panted, "Jackie Robinson...he came up in the third inning and hit a home run." Rickey smiled and lit up a cigar. "And..." the aide continued, "he went four for five.

He Had to Be Protected.

He also stole two bases." Rickey thanked the aide and turned to Red Barber, who was one of his guests that night. "That's a pretty good way to break into organized baseball," he laughed.

Jackie's good spirits from his success that day in Jersey City soon vanished. As the team traveled on the road, he encountered more bad treatment from fans and opposing players than he had expected. In Baltimore he had to be protected from angry fans who waited outside the stadium for him. In Syracuse, New York, an opposing player threw out a live black cat from the dugout, yelling, "Hey Jackie, here's your cousin."

But when Jackie and Rachel got to Montreal, they were pleased to find that the fans were supportive. They had no trouble finding housing, and their neighbors treated them well.

On the road, however, things were different. But Jackie held his temper and played ball. That year he led the International League in hitting with a .349 average. He had the highest fielding percentage for second basemen, even though it was a new position for him. He tied for the lead in scoring and was second in the league in stolen bases. He was named Most Valuable Player in the league.

Led by Jackie, Montreal won the International League pennant by 19 ½ games and represented the league in the Junior World Series against Louisville. Both the town of Louisville and its players were opposed to blacks playing professional ball and they treated Jackie very badly.

The fans hurled abuse at Jackie and the opposing pitchers threw at him. Jackie and the other Royals seemed to feel the intensity of the hate and were able to win only one of the three games played at Louisville.

Back in Montreal, the Royals and Jackie were amazed by their hometown fans' reaction to what

Most Valuable Player

went on in Louisville. Jackie was a very popular player in Montreal, and the fans were furious after reading about what Jackie had endured there. Every Louisville player was booed mercilessly. Jackie received huge cheers. He responded by hitting over .400 for the series. The Royals roared back to win three in a row and take the series.

The fans leaped onto the field, chanting Jackie's name and carrying him and manager Clay Hopper on their shoulders. Jackie was touched but had to slip back into the locker room to dress and catch a plane. When he tried to leave, he was surrounded by a mob of adoring fans. Jackie broke through and ran down the street, the mob pursuing him. Writers at the time remarked that it was the first time a mob of white men pursued a black man with love and not hate in their hearts.

Chapter 12

Breaking the Barrier

In November, 1946, Jackie and Rachel had a lively addition to their family, Jackie Robinson, Jr. Jackie felt proud to give his new son his name. Two other children, Sharon and David, would follow.

Jackie, Jr., was to have a troubled life, and in later years Jackie wondered if he had placed an unfair burden on him by giving his son his own soon-to-be well-known name.

But in November of 1946, Jackie was worried about the more immediate future. Would the

Jackie Waited for the Call.

JACKIE ROBINSON

Dodgers call him up to the big league club for the 1947 season? All through the off-season Jackie waited for the call. But nothing happened.

"Why haven't you purchased Jackie's contract for the Dodgers?" Branch Rickey's son asked him.

"I've got a plan," Branch Rickey responded with a smile. "I'm going to leave Jackie on the Montreal roster during spring training. I'll have the Dodgers play the Royals a lot. When the players on the Dodgers see how good Jackie is, they'll be begging me to sign him up. If they want him on their team, it will make things go a lot smoother."

Rickey decided to hold spring training that year for both the Dodgers and the Royals in Havana, Cuba. He felt there would be less publicity there, and he hoped to avoid the prejudice Jackie had faced in Florida the previous year.

In Cuba, Rickey called Jackie to his side. "Listen, Robinson, I want you to be a whirling demon against the Dodgers. Hit the ball. Get on base any way you can. Run wild. Steal the pants off of them. They're going to demand I put you on the big club!"

The Dodgers played the Royals seven times. In those seven games, Jackie batted .625 and stole seven bases. He had an awesome combination of speed and power. Out on the field, Rickey handed him a first baseman's mitt and told him to learn the new position. Rickey knew the Dodgers were set at second and short, with Eddie Stanky and Pee Wee Reese. The only open position available was first base and Rickey wanted Jackie to learn how to play it.

Despite Jackie's obvious talent, the Brooklyn players didn't respond as Branch Rickey had hoped they would. In fact, the opposite happened. Many of the big leaguers didn't want Jackie on their team, no matter what. Rumors began to spread that they planned to sign a statement saying that they would

Seven bases in Seven Games

refuse to play if the Dodgers promoted Jackie to the team.

Kirby Higbe, a relief pitcher, accidently slipped the news to one of Branch Rickey's aides. The information reached the Dodgers' manager, Leo Durocher. Durocher was a fiercely competitive man, who wanted the Dodgers to win every time they were on the field. For this reason alone, he wanted Jackie on the team. When he heard of the petition, he decided to act right away.

In the middle of the night, Durocher called a team meeting in the kitchen of the hotel the Dodgers were staying in. The sleepy players sat on chopping blocks and counters, leaned against stoves and refrigerators, and listened wide-eyed as their manager shouted at them.

"I hear some of you don't want this fella, Robinson, on the Dodgers," he began. "Well, I'm the manager around here, and I say he plays. I don't care if a guy is yellow or black or striped like a zebra, as long as he can play this game. Robinson can help us win the pennant. And if we win the pennant, we all get richer. And if any one of you doesn't like it, you can expect to be traded."

The next morning, Branch Rickey met individually with the ringleaders of the player revolt. To Carl Furillo, a popular outfielder, Rickey simply said that unless he accepted Jackie, he would be out of a job. Eddie Stanky was a very loyal team player. Rickey called on Stanky's Dodger loyalty and convinced him to accept Jackie.

Hugh Casey, a relief pitcher, and Bobby Bragan, a third-string catcher, were also called into Rickey's office. Rickey told them they had to accept Jackie or be traded.

Rickey had the most trouble with popular outfielder Dixie Walker. Walker was the only player to put his feelings on paper, writing a letter to Rickey

He Decided to Announce the Signing.

asking to be traded. Rickey, ever the astute general manager, could not find a fair trade for Walker, who remained that year with the Dodgers. But Walker was told he would be traded as soon as a good deal could be worked out.

Rickey's plan to have the Dodgers want Jackie on their team had not worked. To make matters worse, the Commissioner of Baseball, Happy Chandler, decided to suspend the Dodger manager, Leo Durocher, for the coming season.

Chandler suspended Durocher for "conduct unbecoming to baseball," claiming that Durocher had associated with known gamblers and gangsters. Rickey decided to act quickly. With the storm of controversy hanging over the Dodgers, he decided to announce the signing of Jackie Robinson to a major-league contract, thinking this news would overwhelm the bad publicity from Durocher's suspension.

JACKIE ROBINSON

On April 9, 1947, the Dodgers issued a one-sentence press release: Brooklyn announces the purchase of the contract of Jack Roosevelt Robinson from Montreal. Signed, Branch Rickey.

With this press release, the color barrier that had prevented blacks from playing major-league baseball had been broken. It was an historic moment. But for the Brooklyn Dodgers and Jackie Robinson, it was a time of terrible turmoil. The Dodgers had just lost their manager and much of the team were uneasy or outright hostile to Jackie.

Jackie Robinson was about to undergo a tremendous ordeal, facing a sometimes hostile press, many prejudiced fans and opposing players. Even his own team was not squarely on his side.

Shortly after Jackie joined the team, Eddie Stanky walked up to him. "I want you to know something," Stanky said, staring directly into Jackie's eyes. "You're on this ball club, and as far I'm

"I Want You to Know Something."

concerned that makes you one of twenty-five players on my team. But before I play with you I want you to know how I feel about it. I want you to know I don't like it. I want you to know I don't like you."

Jackie didn't flinch. He stared right back into Stanky's eyes and replied in a calm, steady voice, "All right. That's the way I'd rather have it. Right out in the open."

The 1947 baseball season was about to begin.

Chapter 13

A Team Grows in Brooklyn

Jackie Robinson, facing the hostility of the opposition and without the support of his teammates, not surprisingly got off to a poor start. In his first game he made out three times, and in his fourth time up was safe only due to an error. In his next four games, he went to bat twenty times without a base hit. He was in a deep slump.

Whispers started that he was overmatched in the big leagues, that he didn't have the talent to play in the majors. Jackie was extremely tense. He

179

"Relax and the Hits Will Fall."

was worried that he would lose his starting job.

Rickey had replaced Durocher with Burt Shotten, an experienced manager whom Jackie had quickly grown to respect. Shotton called him aside. "Jackie, you're putting too much pressure on yourself. I won't take you out of the lineup. Relax and the hits will fall."

But hits were few and far between as the Dodgers began a series with the Philadelphia Phillies. The Phillies' manager, Ben Chapman, was opposed to Jackie's signing, and he encouraged his players to try to intimidate Jackie when he was at bat.

Starting to the plate in the first inning, Jackie could not believe the torrent of abuse he heard from the Phillies' dugout.

"Hey, black boy, why don't you go back to the cotton fields!"

"They're waitin' for you in the African jungles!"

"We don't want you here, black boy!"

JACKIE ROBINSON

"Go back to the bushes!"

Jackie took a deep breath and stepped out of the batter's box. How could he take this abuse and say nothing? How could he just play ball and ignore these insults? In college he was known as a black man who would not tolerate bigotry and racism. How much did Rickey expect of him?

For one moment he thought of going over to the Phillies' dugout, of smashing his fists into the mouths of these ignorant fools. It would feel good to let his emotions take over.

Then he thought of Branch Rickey and Jackie, Jr. He thought of the promise he had made to Rickey. How Rickey had staked his own reputation on Jackie's strong shoulders. He thought of his son, how he would have to tell him that his father could have been the man who broke the color barrier, but had failed.

In the stands, Rachel Robinson tightly gripped

How Much Did Rickey Expect of Him?

the railing of her seat and fought back tears. She was not crying because of the cruel words her husband had to listen to. She was crying because she knew how hard it was for a man as proud as Jackie to hear these words and do nothing.

The usually lively Dodgers' dugout grew silent. Those who had wanted Jackie on their team were angered at the stream of abuse from the Phillies' dugout. But more importantly, those who had opposed Jackie had begun to feel uneasy. There are moments in a person's life when it becomes clear that the way they look at the world is wrong. For many of those Dodgers, who had learned prejudice and bigotry from an early age, this was one of those moments. They could not help but imagine themselves in Jackie's position, hearing all those hateful words.

For Jackie, it was a crossroads. He took another deep breath and made his decision. He didn't even look over at the Phillies' dugout. Without a word, he stepped back into the batter's box and took his turn at bat.

The abuse continued. But in the seventh inning, Jackie struck back—on the field. He lined a sharp single to center field. On the next pitch, he took off for second, stealing it easily. The catcher's throw skipped into center field, and Jackie was up on his feet and sliding into third. Gene Hermanski of the Dodgers followed with a single, and drove Jackie home. That was to prove the deciding run in the Dodger victory.

For the remaining two games of the series, the abuse grew even worse, and still Jackie said and did nothing. As Jackie kicked some dirt from his cleats, he suddenly heard someone shouting back at the Phillies, "Hey, you cowards, why don't you yell at someone who can answer you back?"

To his surprise, Jackie recognized the voice of

Hit by Six Pitches

his defender—Eddie Stanky!

Jackie's rookie season was remarkable—remarkable for his success on the base paths and for the way he handled the abuse and taunts he received.

In his first 37 games, Jackie was hit by pitches six times, and knocked down by brushback pitches nearly every game. In St. Louis, opposing players had almost refused to play against him. In Cincinnati and Boston, opposing fans yelled out curses and threats. The Dodgers' front office received death threats against Jackie. The F.B.I. was brought in to investigate them.

In Chicago, a pitcher tried to pick Jackie off second base. In scrambling back to the base, Jackie's legs got tangled up with the shortstop's, Len Merullo. When Merullo got up, he openly kicked Jackie. Jackie instinctively raised his fist to punch Merullo. But showing amazing self-control, Jackie held back at the last moment.

JACKIE ROBINSON

The Dodgers' chief rivals for the pennant in 1947 were the St. Louis Cardinals. On an easy ground ball, Enos Country Slaughter, a Cardinal player, seemed to spike Jackie deliberately, narrowly missing his Achilles tendon. Jackie did nothing. But his teammates surged out of the dugout in protest, led by Hugh Casey, one of the Dodgers who originally had not wanted Jackie on the team.

Ewell Blackwell, of the Cincinnati Reds, once screamed racial curses at Jackie from the pitcher's mound right after Eddy Stanky had just broken up his no-hitter. Jackie said nothing. He just hit Blackwell's first pitch over the plate into center field for a solid base hit.

Many players around the league began to admire Jackie both for his baseball skills and his courage in keeping his promise to Branch Rickey. Later in that very game against the Cardinals where Slaughter had spiked him, Jackie reached base and spoke to the

His Teammates Surged Out of the Dugout.

Cardinals' star first baseman Stan Musial.

"Stan, if I could, I would really teach those teammates of yours a lesson for messing with me."

"Jackie," Stan responded, "I don't blame you. I just want you to know I'm happy you're playing in this league."

Against the Pittsburgh Pirates, Jackie accidently got tangled up with Pirates slugger Hank Greenberg, and knocked him down. Later in the game when Greenberg reached first, Jackie apologized to him.

Greenberg, who was Jewish, had also encountered bigotry around the league. He told Jackie to keep his head up, and the two men arranged to meet later to discuss their experiences.

But even more important to Jackie than the acceptance he was slowly getting from the opposition, was his growing closeness to his teammates.

Perhaps the most popular Dodger among his

teammates was Pee Wee Reese, the shortstop. Reese came from Louisville, Kentucky. He had grown up in a Southern environment where blacks and whites were always separated. He was at first uneasy about Jackie joining the Dodgers.

In spring training, Dixie Walker had urged Pee Wee to sign his petition. It would have been easy for Pee Wee to sign. Jackie had played shortstop in the Negro Leagues and rumors circulated that he would replace Pee Wee on the Dodgers. But Pee Wee refused.

As the two men got to know each other better, Pee Wee grew to admire Jackie's playing skills and respect his character. On a road trip to Boston, the crowd began to taunt Jackie. Pee Wee looked over at the faces in the crowd, faces full of rage and hate. He looked over at his teammate at first base, enduring the abuse.

Then Pee Wee began to hear curses and shouts

They Were Dodgers—They Were Teammates.

directed toward himself. How could he, a white man, play side by side with Jackie? He was a traitor to his race, they were shouting, he should be ashamed of himself.

Pee Wee called time. He walked over toward Jackie. Jackie looked up in surprise as Pee Wee came toward him. What was happening? Without a glance at the crowd, Pee Wee put his arm around Jackie and said a few words. His words were not significant, his gesture was. With his arm around Jackie, Pee Wee was telling everyone that they were both Dodgers—they were teammates.

Chapter 14

Rookie of the Year

It was a cool night in Pittsburgh in 1947. The Dodgers were in town, playing the Pirates at Forbes Field. The score was 2–2. Jackie Robinson was on third base. He took his usual big lead. He began to dance a bit down the line.

On the mound for the Pirates, Fritz Ostermuller glanced over at Jackie. He remembered the scouting reports he had read before the game. He knew that Jackie liked to disrupt the pitcher's rhythm—that he liked to goad the pitcher into making hurried

His Usual Big Lead

pick-off throws that often skipped past the fielders.

I'm not going to fall into that trap, Ostermuller thought to himself. *I'm not going to let him get the better of me, he's not going anywhere.* Ostermuller decided not to pitch from the stretch position, but to take a full windup.

Eyes ever alert, Jackie noticed Ostermuller go into his full windup, and he took off toward home plate. The crowd leaped to its feet. The Pirates' catcher, intent on the pitch, suddenly noticed Jackie streaking toward home plate.

Arms and legs churning, Jackie raced toward home, and with grace and power slid into the base. The catcher put the tag down, but it was too late. The crowd roared in appreciation. Jackie had stolen home! It was Jackie's most spectacular play in a spectacular season.

Jackie's combination of speed and power added a new dimension to baseball in 1947. He could hit at times with power, belting 12 home runs that year. He could hit for average, hitting .297. He could score, ranking second in the league in runs scored to Johnny Mize, who had slugged over 51 homers that year.

And he could run! Jackie bunted for 19 hits and led the league with 29 steals. The numbers of bunt hits and stolen bases are impressive, but they cannot convey the impact Jackie's base running skills had on the game. Not since Ty Cobb had there been a player who could strike fear into the opposition simply by reaching first base.

Pitchers would pay so much attention to Jackie's antics on the base paths that they would lose concentration. They would throw pitches that were easy to hit, or they would balk, or throw wild pitches or wild pick-off attempts.

In one game that year, Jackie even scored all the way from first on a bunt. Fielders were con-

Jackie Robinson Day at Ebbets Field

stantly out of position, cheating toward the bases, hoping to catch him stealing.

As he danced on the base paths, Jackie would remember Cool Papa Bell's words about bringing the aggressive baserunning game of the Negro Leagues to the major leagues. He remembered Branch Rickey's advice to be a "whirling demon" on the base paths. And he was!

Jackie helped lead the Dodgers past the Cardinals to the National League pennant in 1947. The borough of Brooklyn went wild. The *Sporting News,* which had predicted at the beginning of the season that Jackie would not make it in the big leagues now named him Rookie of the Year.

September 27 was Jackie Robinson Day in Brooklyn. Over 26,000 fans came out to Ebbets Field to salute Jackie. Jackie received gifts and heard speeches praising him from both white and black leaders. Teammates were there to express appreciation and support. It was a storybook ending to a hard and difficult year.

A little later, Jackie and the Dodgers met their crosstown rivals, the powerful New York Yankees, in the World Series. The Yankees were a deeply talented team with players like Joe DiMaggio, Tommy Henrich, Yogi Berra and Phil Rizzuto. The Dodgers lost, four games to three, in a hard-fought series.

It had been a gratifying year for Jackie. He had kept his promise to Branch Rickey and held his tongue and his fists; he had excelled on the field, and his team had reached the World Series. But perhaps most gratifying had been the fact that two other black ballplayers had signed major-league contracts late in the summer—Dan Bankhead for the Dodgers and Larry Doby for the Cleveland Indians.

Branch Rickey's prediction had already started to come true. Jackie Robinson would not be the only

Crosstown Rivals—The New York Yankees

black in baseball. The major leagues would one day be fully integrated.

And not only baseball had changed forever. Within a few years, the other major spectator sports—basketball and football—had become even more quickly integrated than baseball. Black athletes of talent and ability were setting records, attracting fans, and being given financial rewards on the same basis as other professional players.

Chapter 15

A New Jackie

During the off-season, Jackie was invited on many speaking tours, which included testimonial dinners very often. So he did more than speak, he also ate a lot. Leo Durocher was back as manager of the Dodgers at the beginning of 1948, and he was shocked and angered when Jackie reported to camp twenty-five pounds over playing weight.

All through spring training, Leo worked Jackie extra hard, trying to get his excess weight off. But when the regular season opened, neither Jackie nor

Jackie Worked Hard to Stay in Condition.

the Dodgers were ready. Jackie was on the bench, and the Dodgers got off to a very slow start. They had been expected to win the pennant again, but they were going nowhere fast.

Jackie had learned his lesson and worked hard to stay in condition. During the off-season, Eddie Stanky had been traded, so Jackie was able to move to second base, his best position. He and Pee Wee Reese quickly grew used to each other, and they became perhaps the best double-play combination ever.

Jackie's legs and batting eye started to freshen again, too. By the end of the year, his average reached a respectable .296 and he had stolen 22 bases. But the Dodgers limped into third place. It was an all-around disappointing year.

Next year was a different story altogether. Jackie came to 1949 spring training in great shape. The Dodgers were primed and ready for the pennant chase. But most importantly, Branch Rickey had told Jackie the words he had been waiting to hear for three years. "Jackie," Rickey counseled him, "now you're on your own. You can say what you feel."

Jackie wasted no time in letting his personality emerge. He spoke up in the press regarding the second-class accommodations black players had to endure on the road. He spoke out against racial prejudice on and off the field. He criticized sportswriters when he felt they were wrong or inaccurate.

On the field, he began to dispute umpires' calls when he thought they were bad. He verbally defended himself against racial taunts and got into a near fistfight with a prejudiced teammate.

Many sportswriters now began to refer to him as "thin-skinned'"and "arrogant." Jackie believed that unconscious racial prejudice was behind much of the bad press he was starting to get. If a white player protested bad calls, or spoke out, he was

"You Can Say What You Feel."

called competitive or feisty, while a black player was labeled difficult or uppity.

If Jackie was having problems with the press, he certainly wasn't having any problems on the playing fields. He had his highest batting average in 1949—.342. He knocked 16 home runs over the fences, and swiped 37 bases.

Led by Jackie and Pee Wee, the Dodgers reclaimed the pennant and Jackie was named Most Valuable Player in the National League.

The Dodgers again met the New York Yankees in the World Series. The Yankees won another hard-fought series. But with his great personal accomplishments on the field and his new freedom to speak out, Jackie felt that 1949 was the best year of his career.

Chapter 16

Final Innings

In 1950, expectations were high that the Dodgers would repeat as National League champions. But the Philadelphia Phillies—known as the "Whiz Kids"—surged to an early lead.

The Dodgers fought to overcome a huge early lead by the Phillies and almost caught them in September. But the Phillies beat them in a crucial game and took the pennant. Still, Jackie had an impressive year, hitting .328 and stealing 12 bases, and slamming 14 home runs.

Two Younger Black Players Joined the Team.

JACKIE ROBINSON

The Dodgers were changing and so was Jackie's role on the team. Older players were retiring, and younger players were reaching stardom.

Gil Hodges had taken over at first base. He was a brilliant fielder who could also hit for power. Duke Snider, a free-swinging center fielder, had awesome power. Two younger black players had joined the team—Roy Campanella, a chunky power-hitting catcher, and Don Newcombe, a hard-throwing pitcher. Jackie was an older, established player now. He was looked on as a team leader.

But there was some sad news for Jackie in 1950 as well. Branch Rickey, because of financial maneuverings by his partners, had been forced to sell his share of the Brooklyn Dodgers and had moved over to the Pittsburgh Pirates. Walter O'Malley had taken over ownership of the Dodgers. Jackie was seen by O'Malley as a Branch Rickey man. He never had a trusting relationship with O'Malley.

JACKIE ROBINSON

Despite an uncomfortable relationship with the owner, Jackie battled for his team as hard as he could. The following season, 1951, is a famous year in the history of baseball. The Dodgers jumped out to a huge early lead in the pennant chase. But the New York Giants battled back. On the final day of the season the Giants won their game. The Dodgers would have to win to force a playoff.

The Dodgers played the Phillies in their final game. The Phillies took an early 6–1 lead, but the Dodgers battled back to force an 8–8 tie. The game went into extra innings.

In the bottom of the twelfth, with two outs and the bases loaded, a Phillies player hit a sharp line drive up the middle. Jackie, playing second base, was shaded over toward first. It was a sure hit. But at the last moment, Jackie leaped to his right and caught the ball in the tip of his glove. As he fell over, he jammed his right hand into the turf, nearly

At the Last Minute

knocking himself out.

His teammates wondered if Jackie could continue to play. He was in terrible pain. But continue he did, and in the top of the fourteenth inning he hit a home run to win the game. The Dodgers had finished the regular season tied with the Giants. The two New York teams were baseball's greatest rivals.

They split the first two games of the playoffs. In the third and deciding game, Jackie drove in the first run, and scored the Dodgers' third run, giving them a 3–1 lead going into the bottom of the ninth.

But in the ninth, the Giants' Bobby Thomson hit a three-run homer to give the Giants the game. Thomson's home run—known as the "Shot Heard Round the World"—stunned the Dodger fans. Films of the game show Jackie following Thomson around the base paths, checking to see if Thomson touched every base. Afterward, Jackie was the only Dodger to go over to the Giants' clubhouse to congratulate them on their victory.

Despite the disappointment of the final game, 1951 was another superb year for Jackie. He hit .338 with a career-high 19 home runs, and stole 25 bases. His teammate Roy Campanella was named Most Valuable Player. Some people think that only Jackie's poor relationship with the press prevented him from winning his second MVP award.

In 1952 and 1953, the Dodgers won the pennants. But each year they were defeated by the Yankees in the World Series. "Wait 'til next year" was the rallying cry of the Dodgers and their fans. Each year the World Series just seemed to elude their grasp. But despite not winning the ultimate title, the Dodgers' teams during these years accomplished much.

Those years between 1949 and 1953 were successful for Jackie as well. He hit for an average of .329, drove in 463 runs, scored 540 runs and stole 115 bases. During these years, with his production

Whitey Ford Tried to Ignore Jackie.

at the plate and his leadership qualities, he became recognized as one of the great players of the game.

By 1954, Jackie's skills had begun to diminish. The Dodgers had a new manager, Walt Alston, with whom Jackie didn't get along. The Dodgers didn't do well that year either; Jackie played only 124 games. In 1955 the Dodgers came back to win the pennant. Once again they faced the Yankees in the World Series. The Yankees took a lead in the opening game. In the eighth inning, with the Dodgers still trailing, an older, heavier, slower Jackie Robinson found himself on third base. Jackie danced off the base, just as he had so many times before.

He bluffed going. He stopped and started. Whitey Ford, pitching for the Yankees, tried to ignore Jackie. After all, everyone knew Jackie was no longer the base-stealing threat he had once been. But on Ford's second pitch, Jackie took off. From somwhere deep inside him, he summoned the speed of yesterday and with a beautiful hook slide, beat Yogi Berra's tag. Jackie had stolen home again!

The Yankees won that game, but Jackie had sent a message. This time the Dodgers were not to be denied. They went on to win the World Series. Jackie got his first and only Championship ring.

1956 was Jackie's last year in baseball. He had become a part-time player. But as the season wore on, Alston decided to play Jackie more often. He responded and helped lead the Dodgers to yet another pennant.

There was no magic in the World Series this year, however, except for the Yankees. Don Larsen pitched a perfect game, the only one in World Series history, and the Yankees went on to win the series.

In the off season of 1956, the Dodgers traded Jackie to the Giants. But Jackie had already decided to retire. He had played for ten years, had led his team to numerous league championships and

Jackie Had Stolen Home Again!

had put together impressive lifetime statistics.

Jackie Robinson remains one of the all-time major league leaders in stealing home. He averaged .311 for his career and won the Rookie of The Year and Most Valuable Player awards. More importantly, however, by this time many young black players were now in the major leagues. The hope and promise in the handshake between Jackie Robinson and Branch Rickey had started to come true. Things were changing, though not as fast as Jackie would have liked them to.

Chapter 17

After Baseball

Even before he was traded to the Giants, Jackie Robinson had already decided to retire after the 1956 season. Neither his teammates nor Dodger management knew that Jackie Robinson was suffering from diabetes, a serious illness. Jackie realized he no longer had his trademark blazing speed. His bat had slowed and he had trouble getting around on the good fastball pitchers. Still, Jackie was hurt that the team he had played so hard for, did not want him to finish his career with them.

Life After Baseball

JACKIE ROBINSON

Players had very little control of their careers at this time. They could be traded at any time and were not able to sign up with the team of their choice when their contracts were up—they were not free agents. Years later, when an outfielder named Curt Flood challenged the baseball owners in court on this issue, Jackie Robinson offered his support.

But by 1956, Jackie had little interest in continuing his career with any baseball team. For many players, retiring from the playing field is the saddest moment of their lives. After the glory and fame of their playing days, everything afterward seems dull and pointless. Not so for Jackie Robinson. He wanted to and succeeded in having an important and exciting life after baseball.

Jackie went to work for Chock Full O' Nuts, a restaurant chain. These restaurants employed mostly black counterpeople. Jackie had long discussions with William Black, the owner of the restaurant chain. He made it clear that he wanted a position where he could make a real contribution to the company and its workers, that he did not want to be hired simply because he had been a famous baseball player.

Jackie took the job because he could have an important role, helping the management succeed financially while insuring the staff was well taken care of.

While working at the restaurants, Jackie became involved in political concerns. As a well-known black American, Jackie was a valuable personality to have on one's side, and both presidential candidates in the 1960 election, John F. Kennedy and Richard Nixon, actively asked for Jackie's support. He decided to campaign for then Vice President Nixon.

After Nixon was defeated, Jackie became close to another powerful Republican Party figure, Nel-

Jackie Campaigned With Richard Nixon

son Rockefeller, then Governor of New York State. Jackie supported Rockefeller in his drive for the presidency in 1964.

Most black Americans supported Democratic rather than Republican party candidates. But Jackie was always very independent, and did not mind some of the criticism he received from other black leaders for supporting a Republican. He felt it was crucial for black people to have good relations with both major political parties.

After Rockefeller lost to Barry Goldwater, Jackie switched his allegiance to President Johnson, the Democratic Party candidate. With the Republican Party growing more politically conservative, Jackie rejoined the Democrats. Yet he retained close personal relations with many Republican Party leaders, often writing them letters on important issues.

Jackie also became involved with the civil rights movement. He worked with organizations

JACKIE ROBINSON

like the NAACP and Southern Christian Leadership Conference (SCLC) chaired by Dr. Martin Luther King, Jr.

In the summer of 1963, Dr. King and his followers were being savagely treated by Bull Connor, the sheriff of Birmingham, Alabama, as they campaigned for their civil rights. Jackie used his fame and popularity to raise money for Dr. King. But as news footage of the demonstrations showed more and more brutal acts by the Birmingham police, Jackie told his family he must be there to support Dr. King in person.

Jackie flew to Birmingham and delivered a rousing introduction for Dr. King in a packed church. Jackie spoke about the violence of the police and the courage of the demonstrators. He spoke of the pride the entire black community had in the demonstrators who risked their safety to demonstrate for freedom.

Jackie Worked With Martin Luther King, Jr.

Times were changing. Young blacks could openly speak out against racial injustice. They no longer had to endure the restraints Jackie felt in his first years in baseball. And Jackie was there to support them.

Jackie himself had been an inspiration to Martin Luther King, Jr. Dr. King once told a close friend, "Jackie Robinson made it possible for me in the first place. Without him, I would never have been able to do what I did."

Many in the black community appreciated Jackie's efforts on behalf of the civil rights movement. Earlier in 1962, the SCLC sponsored a testimonial dinner for Jackie, at which Dr. King spoke. He thanked Jackie for all the work he had done on his organization's behalf. Telegrams were read from black and white leaders. It was one of Jackie's proudest moments.

Two weeks later another event made Jackie

very proud as well. In his first year of eligibility, Jackie was voted by the baseball writers to the Hall of Fame. As he accepted the honor, Jackie called to the podium the three most important people in his life, Rachel, his loyal and devoted wife; Mallie, his mother; and Branch Rickey. The first black man to play in the major leagues was officially acknowledged as one of the all-time greats.

Jackie also was named to the board of directors of the Freedom National Bank, the first black-owned bank in the United States. Jackie felt that a minority-owned bank could help support black businesses and offer loans to deserving individuals in the black community. He was proud of his work in supporting the bank. Then rumors came about that the bank was being poorly managed. Jackie began an investigation that uncovered some bad banking practices. With the help of others, he reestablished trust in the bank.

The Three Most Important People

JACKIE ROBINSON

But not all went well for the Robinson family. Jackie Robinson, Jr. served during the Vietnam war. When he got back from the service, he was addicted to drugs. His addiction spiraled out of control until he was arrested in New York in 1967. Jackie and Rachel quickly hurried to him. Surrounded by reporters eager for his reaction, Jackie shook his head and sadly said, "I guess I had more of an effect on other people's kids then I had on my own." Jackie, Jr. was sent to a rehabilitation center to help him try to overcome his problems.

As a baseball player often on the road, and then as a community leader, Jackie had spent many hours away from home. He felt guilty that perhaps he had not given Jackie, Jr. the attention he needed. But during the next few years Jackie devoted most of his energy to helping his son overcome his problems. The two grew closer than they had ever been before.

Jackie also became very aware of the drug problem that affects so many young people in both black and white communities. He campaigned for more funding for drug rehabilitation programs and more anti-drug education.

Jackie, Jr. overcame his addiction and began to work as a drug counselor himself. Then, tragically, he was killed in a car accident in 1971. Jackie and Rachel were terribly grieved. But Jackie would proudly point out that Jackie, Jr. had been clean for three years before his death.

In a speech to troubled youngsters shortly before his death, Jackie Jr., told his listeners, "My father was always in my corner. I didn't always recognize that and I didn't always call on him, but he was always there."

Diabetes can be a very dangerous disease, and in his later years, Jackie began to suffer. His legs

No Dodger Would Ever Wear That Number.

swelled and he lost the sight in one eye. It was a frail man, looking much older than his 53 years, who walked on to the field to thunderous applause in 1972 at Dodger Stadium for Jackie Robinson Day. The Dodgers, now playing in Los Angeles, were retiring Jackie's uniform number—42. No Dodger player could ever wear that number again.

Later that year, just before the start of the second game of the World Series, Jackie was honored by baseball for the twenty-fifth anniversary of his first season. As he spoke to the crowd, Jackie told them how pleased he was to be there, then paused and continued, "I will be more pleased the day I can look over at the third-base line and see a black man as manager." Jackie never stopped fighting for what he believed in.

A few months later, on October 24, 1972, Jackie Robinson died. His funeral was held in New York's Riverside Church. Jesse Jackson delivered the eulogy, calling Jackie the "black knight who check-mated bigotry." Richard Nixon and Nelson Rockefeller as well as the mayor of New York City were in attendance. Great athletes like Hank Aaron and Joe Louis came to honor Jackie. And of course, his former Dodger teammates, Carl Erskine, Don Newcombe, Roy Campanella and Pee Wee Reese were there.

Rachel Robinson had requested that many seats should be available to ordinary people who wanted to attend, working people in Harlem and schoolchildren. Though Jackie had lived many years in almost daily contact with famous and wealthy people inside and outside of sports, he and Rachel always remembered where they had come from.

The Jackie Robinson story remains a story of hope and promise—a promise we must all continue to work toward. Recently, a young minor-league prospect named Butch Huskey was called up to the

A Story of Hope and Promise

JACKIE ROBINSON

New York Mets. He asked that he be given number 42 for his uniform, in tribute to Jackie Robinson. When asked what he would say to Jackie, were he able to meet him, the young man answered, "Thank you!"